EXPOSITIO

MISSAE

EXPOSITIO MISSAE

THE MYSTERIES OF THE MASS EXPLAINED

SAINT BONAVENTURE

Translated by Fr. Robert Nixon, OSB

TAN Books
Gastonia, North Carolina

Translated by Fr. Robert Nixon, OSB

Cover design by Jordan Avery

Cover image: Mass for the Order of Trinitarians, 1666 (oil on canvas) by Don Juan Carreno de Miranda (1614-85). Bridgeman Images

ISBN: 978-1-5051-3250-2
Kindle ISBN: 978-1-5051-3466-7
ePUB ISBN: 978-1-5051-3465-0

Published in the United States by
TAN Books
PO Box 269
Gastonia, NC 28053
www.TANBooks.com

Printed in the United States of America

"Thou didst feed thy people with the food of angels, and gavest them bread from heaven prepared without labor; having in it all that is delicious, and the sweetness of every taste."

WISDOM 16:20

CONTENTS

TRANSLATOR'S NOTE

The Mass is a central and essential part of the Christian life, the very source and summit of our devotion and piety. Instituted by Jesus Himself at the Last Supper and faithfully passed on by the apostles and their successors, it is not merely a memorial of the passion, death, and resurrection of Our Savior, but a true participation in His one redeeming sacrifice. It does not merely praise and invoke God, but causes Him to be really, truly, and substantially present. It is through the Mass that we become closest to Jesus and mystically partake in His passion, death, and resurrection. It is through the Mass that we receive the "Bread of the Angels," which imparts to our fragile human nature the eternal life of God Himself.

It is not surprising that many commentaries on the Mass have been written over the years. But the one which merits primacy of place is that produced by Saint Bonaventure. Bonaventure of Bagnoregio (1221–1274), deservedly known as the Seraphic Doctor, was a great Franciscan mystic and scholastic theologian. As well as serving as seventh Minister-General of the Franciscans, he was an outstanding theologian, philosopher, preacher, teacher, and poet. His voluminous writings combine vast erudition and outstanding intelligence with a radiant mystical insight and an unmistakable sanctity and humility.

His *Expositio Missae* (literally "Exposition of the Mass") offers inspiring and touching insight into the multiple layers of meaning and symbolism embodied within the sacred actions of the Eucharistic celebration. It is to be noted that the Mass has changed in certain details over the centuries. Nevertheless, the texts and actions described by Bonaventure correspond very closely to the Tridentine Mass, also known as the Traditional Latin Mass. This Mass was not, of course, a new invention following the Council of Trent, but a faithful compilation and harmonization of the traditions which had already been in existence for many centuries. Having said that, before the availability of printed Missals, there was an inevitable minor degree of variation in numerous particular details. For this reason, there are certain instances where Bonaventure's descriptions differ slightly from the Tridentine Missal.

To appreciate Bonaventure's commentary most fruitfully, a familiarity with the texts and rubrics of the Traditional Latin Mass will be extremely helpful. However, readers who are only acquainted with the *Novus Ordo* will also be able to follow his explanations without substantial difficulty, especially if they are able to consult the Tridentine Missal. Of course, the text he refers to is the Roman Canon, identified in the *Novus Ordo* Missal as Eucharistic Prayer I, and which was *the* Eucharistic Prayer of the Latin Rite Church from late antiquity until the latter part of the twentieth century.

In preparing this translation, words and phrases in Latin and English have been freely juxtaposed as suits the specific context, since some of the explanations offered only make sense in relation to the original Latin text. Footnotes or parenthetical interpolations providing translations (and other useful or interesting details) have been added by the translator. Often Bonaventure will quote only the beginning of a passage from the Mass or from Scripture, assuming that his readers would know the text which follows by heart. In such cases, the complete text has been inserted for the benefit of the modern reader.

Offered also in this volume are some of the Seraphic Doctor's beautiful and passionate prayers—namely, those to be said before Mass, before the reception of Holy Communion, and after Mass. The first two are taken from his *De Preparatione ad Missam,* and the last one is a well-known prayer included in many older breviaries.

It is the hope of the translator that this work will be found inspiring, instructive, and illuminating; and, above all, that it may achieve Bonaventure's own stated goal—namely, that of helping his readers "to hear the most holy Mass with the greatest possible devotion and reverence." For in doing this, we are being brought into ever deeper union with Our Lord and Savior, Jesus Christ; Who, with the Father and the Holy Spirit, lives and reigns forever and ever. Amen.

Fr. Robert Nixon, OSB,
Abbey of the Most Holy Trinity,
New Norcia, Western Australia

SAINT BONAVENTURE'S PRAYER BEFORE MASS

Behold, O heavenly Father! I offer to You this sacrifice of praise. As I do so, I reflect upon the death of Your only begotten Son, Our Lord Jesus Christ. Truly, this is the same sacrifice which He Himself offered for my salvation and for the salvation of all the world. Behold, I bear this living offering to the altar of Your Majesty, which is the very same offering which You made upon the altar of the cross for our sake!

O heavenly Father, recall that sacred perspiration which Your Son shed in His anxiety, and which flowed to the ground like great drops of blood. Look upon that immaculate flesh, cruelly struck with blows, bruised with slaps and clubs, discolored with wounds, dishonored by spittle, reddened by His freely flowing blood, pierced by the spikes of His crown of thorns, affixed to the wood of the cross by nails, and finally wounded with the spear which opened His sacred side.

May that same divine mercy, which drove Your Son to hang from the gibbet of the cross as the price of our liberty, impel You also, heavenly Father, to take pity on us. Look not upon our sins, but on the face of Your beloved Son! For we seek forgiveness and pardon not by virtue of the multitude of our prayers, but rather through the grace of Your great mercy. *Amen.*

EXPOSITION OF THE MASS

1

THE VESTMENTS OF THE PRIEST AND THEIR MEANINGS

The apostle Saint Paul, in his Epistle to the Hebrews, speaks of "Christ standing as our High Priest."[1] For He is indeed our true High Priest. And so immense is Christ's priestly dignity that everything which bishop and priests do in the celebration of Mass represents Him in some manner. As I know that you, O Reader, wish to hear the most holy Mass with the greatest possible devotion and reverence, I shall write to you on what the words and actions of the Mass signify, and how they represent the person and actions of Our Lord Jesus Christ.

It is to be noted that firstly the priest puts on the *amice*. This item, which extends to the shoulders, is regarded as one of the sacred vestments. Following this, he robes himself with an *alb*, and girdles himself with a *cincture*. He then places a *manipple*

---

1 Hebrews 9:11.

over his left arm. He then drapes a long *stole* around his neck, and finally puts on the *chasuble.*

We will briefly explain what each of these vestments signify. The amice, covering the upper body, represents Christ as Head of the Church, Who concealed His divinity beneath the veil of His humanity.

The alb, which is white and clean, signifies the purity of Christ, of Whom Saint Peter said, "He committed no sin, and there was no deception to be found in His mouth."[2] Such cleanness from the stain of sin is imparted by Christ to each one of us through the sacrament of Baptism. The linen fabric of the alb is made clean by washing it in water, corresponding to the purifying action of the waters of the baptismal font.

The cincture symbolizes the virginity of both Christ and His most chaste Mother. Our Lord similarly exhorts us all to cultivate such chastity and purity, insofar as we are able, when He said, "Let your loins be girded!"[3]

The maniple, placed on the left arm, symbolizes the humility and meekness of Christ during His earthly life. But it also signifies His readiness for battle and His courage in combat. For Our Lord indeed fought bravely for justice and truth, and He single-handedly conquered the world and overturned the dominion of the devil. In this regard, the maniple may be viewed as a representation of a shield, equipping the one who bears

---

2 1 Peter 2:22.

3 Luke 12:35.

it for battle for the sake of justice. And Christ urged us to be ready for such warfare, when He said, "Blessed are those who suffer persecution for the sake of justice."[4]

The long stole, which is placed around the neck and hangs before the heart and then extends to the feet, signifies the obedience of Christ and His voluntary servitude for the sake of our salvation. For He, so that He might save us from eternal damnation, "became obedient to the Father unto death, even death on the cross."[5] This is symbolized by the form of the cross, which is customarily embroidered onto the stole where it passes over the chest. The design of the cross over the heart of the priest serves to remind all the assembly that we also ought to carry the passion of Christ in our heart at all times.

The chasuble (*casula*), which means literally "a small house," (*parva casa*) signifies Christ as filling both heaven and earth, just as He declared through the prophet, "Heaven and earth I have filled."[6] It also symbolizes the all-encompassing charity with which we ought to love our friends *in* God, and our enemies *because of* God. Christ taught us this holy lesson both by word and by example. For in the Gospel of Matthew, it is recorded that He said, "Love your enemies, and pray for those who persecute you."[7]

---

4 Matthew 5:10.

5 Philippians 2:8.

6 Jeremiah 23:24.

7 Matthew 5:44.

2

THE MEANING OF THE NAME "MASS" AND THE INTRODUCTORY RITES

The celebration of the holy Sacrament of the altar is called the "Mass," and is related to the word "mission" (or sending forth).[8] For the Mass is like a legation sent forth between God and humanity, and between humanity and God. For God sends His only begotten Son, Jesus Christ, to the altar. And the Church, in turn, offers this same Christ back to the almighty Father, as she intercedes on behalf of sinners for the salvation of the world.

In accordance with this, the priest pronounces an act of contrition before celebrating the Mass. For although he acts as a herald and legate of the faithful, he ought to acknowledge himself also to be a sinner. Therefore, he should not hesitate to recognize his own imperfections and failings, according to the

[8] In Latin, *Missa* is the past participle of *Mittere* ("to send").

wisdom of the verse, "The just man is his own accuser."[9] This act of contrition of the priest before Mass reflects and highlights that fact that "Christ died for sinners, the just One for the unjust, so that He might offer us to God."[10]

Similarly, Christ said (speaking through the psalmist), "The words of sinners are far from My salvation!"[11] It is as if He proclaims here, "The sins and iniquities of My people will not permit Me to live; so it is only fitting that I should die for these afflicted and suffering sinners. For it is only thus that I may reconcile them to My heavenly Father, and offer them to Him for the sake of His eternal glory."

Following this, the priest approaches the altar and kisses it. By this action, he signifies that salvation and peace have been announced to both the Jews and the Gentiles who are converted to faith in Christ, through the incarnation and passion of the same Christ. For the altar possesses two sides, or two corners. The right corner of the altar signifies the Jews; and the left corner represents the Gentiles. Hence it is that the Mass commences at the right corner, for it was out of the people of the Jews that Christ accepted His humanity. For the Blessed Virgin Mary was born of the royal house of David. And it was

---

9 Proverbs 18:17.

10 1 Peter 3:18.

11 Psalm 21:2. The quoted verse is *Longe a salute mea verba peccatorum meorum*. The sense which Bonaventure gives to it here differs from most modern translations.

she who, by the Holy Spirit, conceived Christ the Lord in His incarnate Body.

Then the choir or the priest begin the Introit, which all the clergy present should sing together harmoniously. For the word *choir* means, in Greek, "harmoniously." This Introit is customarily sung twice. The practice of singing the Introit twice signifies the desire for the coming of the Savior of the ancient fathers (which includes both the company of prophets and the patriarchs). In the person of this twofold group of ancient fathers, Isaiah spoke of the incarnation of Christ (for which both the prophets and the patriarchs had yearned for so earnestly) when he proclaimed, "Would that You would rend the heavens, and descend!"[12]

And at last, hearing this heartfelt clamor, the merciful Lord came into the world. It was of this coming into the world that He spoke, when He prophesied through the psalmist, "Now I shall arise, on account of the misery of the afflicted and the weeping of the poor."[13]

Another reason why the Introit is sung twice is that it designates that the One Who was to come would have a twofold nature, being both divine and human, in one and the same person.

Yet another reason for the singing of the Introit twice is that it means that the "Glory be to the Father. . ." occurs both in

---

[12] Isaiah 64:1.

[13] Psalm 11:6.

the *middle* of the singing, and at the *end* (that is, it appears both at the ending of the Introit the first time it is sung, and it appears again at the ending of its repetition). The occurrence of the Trinitarian doxology in the middle signifies that Christ entered into the midst of the world (or into "the middle" of our human condition) through the Virgin, and thereby revealed to us the mystery of the Holy Trinity. Yet He also taught this same mystery at the *end* of His earthly sojourn, by manifesting the splendor and eternal unity of the Father, Son, and Holy Spirit, by His glorious ascension into heaven.

Many of the saints have imitated this twofold affirmation of the mystery of the Trinity. For, like Christ, they entered into the world through physical birth. Through the sacrament of Baptism, they are born a second time into the faith of the Trinity; or through the shedding of their blood for the sake of Christ, they have come to be mystically reborn in the Trinitarian faith, as companions to the angels in heaven.[14]

The verses imploring the mercy of the Lord (i.e., the *Kyrie eleison*) are then sung, including a ninefold repetition of our humble petition for mercy.[15] This ninefold repetition is connected to the parable of the lost drachma, and relates particular-

---

[14] In the original, this point is somewhat obscure. The translation has been adapted slightly to make the point which Bonaventure is making slightly clearer.

[15] That is, *Kyrie eleison* is sung three times, then *Christe eleison* is sung three times, and then *Kyrie eleison* is sung a further three times, giving a ninefold invocation of the mercy of God. In the *Novus Ordo* Missal, each verse is repeated only twice, not thrice.

ly to the tenth drachma, which was misplaced.[16] This lost tenth drachma symbolizes our human nature, which (like the coin in the parable) had been lost. The nine other coins, which were not lost (signified by the ninefold repetition in the *Kyrie*), signify the nine choirs of holy angels. This ninefold imploring of God's mercy expresses the hope that the lost tenth drachma (signifying our fallen human nature) should be restored to the nine which were not lost (that is, that we should be placed in the glorious company of the nine choirs of angels).

Because of this symbolic reference to the nine choirs of angels in the *Kyrie,* the hymn sung by the angels, the *Gloria in excelsis Deo,* follows next. It was this hymn which the angelic multitude proclaimed so jubilantly at the nativity of Christ.[17] This chant is commenced by the priest, who represents Christ. This signifies that Our Lord willed to become incarnate for the sake of the restoration of the human race.

The text of this hymn, which follows the words sung by the angels (that is, from the *Laudamus te*[18] until the end), is believed by some to have been written by the blessed Pope Telesphorus,[19] who was eighth in succession as Bishop of Rome after Saint Peter. However, there are others who hold the view that

---

16 See Luke 15:8–10.

17 See Luke 2:14.

18 "We praise You."

19 Died 137.

it was written by Saint Hilary,[20] the bishop of Poitiers, and an important teacher in the early Church.

It should be understood that when we sing the *Kyrie,* we implore the mercy of the Lord in a Trinitarian fashion. For in the first *Kyrie eleison,* we mean, "O Lord, God and Father, have mercy on us." In the second invocation, *Christe eleison,* it is as if we fervently cry out, "Our Lord Jesus Christ, Son of David, have mercy on us." And the final *Kyrie eleison* signifies, "O Lord, Holy Spirit, have mercy on us."

Thus the overall mystical sense of the *Kyrie* is:

Holy Father, Who sent Your Son that He should be born of the Virgin Mary, have mercy on us, so that we may be united with the nine choirs of angels;

Christ, Son of the living God, Who deigned to be born of the Virgin Mary, have mercy on us;

Holy Spirit, Who filled the Virgin Mary with Your grace when she conceived Christ, have mercy on us.

In this way, the *Kyrie* serves to invoke mercy from the entire Trinity.

We then follow this (as has been noted) with the *Gloria in excelsis.* By this glorious hymn, we make it clear that we worship and adore the same God here on earth as the angels do in heaven.

After this follows the opening prayer, which is called the *Collect.* It is given this name because it indicates that all present

---

[20] 310–367.

at the celebration of the liturgy ought, at this point, to collect diligently their thoughts and intentions, and join in prayer in union with the priest.

But before the prayer has come a salutation of the people, namely *Dominus vobiscum* (or "The Lord be with you"). This form is used when the Mass is celebrated by a presbyter (or priest). But a bishop, because he is a vicar of Christ, customarily uses that form of salutation with which the resurrected Christ greeted His disciples, namely *Pax vobiscum* (or "Peace be with you").[21] This episcopal salutation carries the sense, "If you will to be present worthily for the celebration of these Mysteries, then may you be sons of peace!"

Concerning the salutation used by ordinary priests, that is *Dominus vobiscum,* the people respond *Et cum spiritu tuo* (or, "And with your spirit"). As Saint Jerome observes, this reflects the fact that the Spirit of God desires to be with the human spirit, for it is the rational spirit dwelling within a person which makes him human, and causes him to be the image and likeness of the divinity.

The priest urges all present to prayer by saying *Oremus* ("Let us pray") at the beginning of the Collect. When we hear this, we should put aside all vain and useless thoughts; we should dismiss from our hearts and minds every trace of detraction, grumbling and gossip, and attend most diligently to the prayer spoken by the priest. For the priest gathers and unites the

21 See John 20:21, 26.

prayers and intentions of all those present, and pours out supplication before God on behalf of the whole assembly. When he reaches the conclusion of this prayer, he humbly beseeches that he may merit to be heard by the Father "through Our Lord Jesus Christ."

3

THE LITURGY OF THE WORD

If we wish our prayers to be heard, it behooves us, in turn, to listen carefully to the Lord crying out to us in the readings of Scripture, and endeavor to fulfill the instructions we receive from these.

The reading before the Gospel is referred to as "the Epistle." Sometimes this reading is taken from the Old Testament and at other times from the New Testament. For both the Old Testament and the New Testament communicate to us truths about God, and His law and wisdom. It is called the *Epistola* from *epi* (which means "above"), and *stola* (which means "a sending forth," similar to the word *Missa*). For all the prophets and apostles who composed the Sacred Scriptures of both Testaments spoke under the inspiration of the Holy Spirit,[22] and thus a message from above was sent by means of their words.

---

22 See 2 Peter 1:21.

It should be noted that on the fourth day of the week (that is, Wednesday) in each of the 'four times' [i.e., the Wednesdays of the four sets of Ember days, that is after the Third Sunday of Advent, the First Sunday of Lent, Pentecost Sunday, and the Feast of the Exaltation of the Holy Cross], two readings are used: one from the prophets and one from the New Testament letters. This practice indicates that all who are ordained into the priestly Orders ought to be learned in both the Old and the New Testaments. The use of two readings also signifies that they ought to be clean and pure in the two aspects which constitute the human person, that is, in body and in soul.

In previous times, clerics preparing for ordination to the priesthood would be examined over the days from Wednesday until Saturday, and then presented to the bishop. On this Saturday, five readings would be read at the Mass. This practice illustrated that all who were making themselves ready for ordination ought to be illuminated in all of their five senses (that is to say, fully illuminated), so that they would be well equipped to rule the people entrusted to their pastoral care. For otherwise, they would be merely "the blind leading the blind."[23]

The faithful people present at the Mass should be diligent in persevering faithfully in all the precepts of the Lord which are heard in the readings. The *Graduale* [that is, the chant sung after the Epistle reading, and before the *Alleluia*] indicates that they ought to progress from virtue to virtue, continually walking in

---

[23] Matthew 15:14.

the path of the commandments. For the word *Graduale* comes from *gradiendo,* which means "by taking steps." Hence it is that the Lord admonishes us, "If you wish to enter into life, then persevere in keeping the commandments."[24]

The *Graduale* is concluded after two verses. These two verses signify that it is upon the twofold precept of charity (namely, love of God and love of neighbor) that "the entire law and prophets depend."[25]

It is through this twofold charity that we will merit the joys of the celestial kingdom. Such joys are represented by the "Alleluia," which follows the *Graduale.* For the souls of the blessed in heaven will praise God without cessation, and the word *Alleluia* means "Praise the Lord!" The joys of these souls in heaven, which are expressed in the praise, are said to be endless and ineffable. Hence, it is that the final syllable of the *Alleluia* is sung with great sweetness, and sustained in a protracted fashion. For, customarily, when we sing this *Alleluia,* the final *a* is intoned through an extended melisma, or long series of notes. By doing this, it is as if we are representing in sound the endless and ineffable joy of the saints in heaven, who exalt in the eternal praise of God.

But in times of sorrow [such as in the seasons of Lent and Septuagesima, and at funeral and requiem Masses], a *Tract* is sung in place of the *Alleluia*. If the *Alleluia* expresses the eternal

---

[24] Matthew 19:17.

[25] Matthew 22:40.

joys of heaven, the Tract, which replaces it in certain seasons and on certain occasions, reflects the manifold sorrows and miseries of this present world.

We now will speak of *Sequences.* The name "Sequence" means "something which follows," for the Sequence follows the ancient chant of the *Alleluia* (or, as the case may be, the Tract). The form of the Sequence was first created by Notker, the Abbot of the monastery of Saint Gall.[26]

Today, the "grey monks" [that is, monks of the Order of Tiron] do not include Sequences in their liturgies; for they do not follow the ancient practices in their singing.[27] After Notker of Saint Gall, many others composed additional sequences. A prominent composer of sequences was Hermanus Contractus [or Herman the Lame], who wrote the *Ave Præclara* and *Sancti Spiritus,* and many others, of which it would be too lengthy to make mention.[28]

Before the Gospel is proclaimed, the words *Sequentia sancti Evangelii* ["What follows is from the holy Gospel"] are said. In

---

26 In his text, Bonaventure gives the name as "Natherus." However, this was an alternate form of the name Notker, which is more commonly used. There was a Notker who was Abbot of the monastery of Saint Gall in the tenth century. However, the creation of the Sequence is attributed to a different Notker (Notker Balbulus, or Notker the Stammerer), who was a monk (but not abbot) of the same monastery in the ninth century. The collection of Sequences composed by this Notker survives to this day.

27 The Order of Tiron was a French monastic order, founded in 1106. It continued to exist until 1627, when it was amalgamated with the Benedictines.

28 Hermanus Contractus is believed by many scholars to have written the *Salve Regina.*

others words, the reading which follows will be taken from one of the holy Gospels; or, more specifically, from the words of either Matthew or John.[29]

It behooves us to consider now why the Gospel is always read in the northern side of the Church,[30] and what this practice signifies. The Greek word *Evangelium* means "Good News." And what could possibly be better news for humanity than what the Son of God, sent by the Father, announced, "Come, ye blessed of My Father; inherit the kingdom prepared for you since the foundation of the world!"?[31]

The fact that the Gospel is read toward the northern part of the Church signifies that the Lord Jesus, Who deigned to be made flesh for our sake, came to dispel and overthrow Lucifer and all the demonic powers of the air. For this, Lucifer himself audaciously and presumptuously declared, "I shall place my throne toward the north, I will be similar to the Most High."[32] But in response, he was told, "You shall be brought down to the hell, and cast down into the depths of the abyss!"[33]

---

29 At the time when Bonaventure was writing, the Gospel reading at Mass was always taken from either the Gospel according to Matthew or the Gospel according to John.

30 The Gospel is customarily read on the left side of the altar. Assuming that the church is constructed so that Mass is said facing the east (in accordance with ancient tradition), this would mean that it is read from the northern side of the altar.

31 Matthew 25:34.

32 Isaiah 14:13–14.

33 Isaiah 14:15.

Therefore, the Gospel is read toward the north, so that (figuratively) the north wind may be dispelled, and the south wind may come[34]—this is to say, so that the devil and his minions may be put to flight and the Holy Spirit come upon us.

The minister who is reading the Gospel customarily greets the people first, to wish for them blessings and salvation of the Lord [by saying, "The Lord be with you"]. By this, it is hoped that the hearts and minds of those present may be opened to hearing and fulfilling the words of the holy Gospel. At the conclusion of the Gospel reading, the people respond, "Glory to You, O Lord!" This carries the full sense of, "Glory to You, O Lord, Who have deigned to call us to Your divine teaching, and to redeem us from death and sin by Your precious Blood."

At the commencement of the Gospel reading, the faithful who are present, together with the minister who is to read the Gospel, all sign themselves with the sign of the holy cross. They do this in order to consecrate themselves for hearing the words which follow attentively and intelligently, and also to dispel from their minds all distracting and superfluous thoughts. By doing this, they hopefully render themselves worthy to merit to hear those wonderful words which Our Lord once spoke to His faithful disciples, "You are clean, because of the word which I have spoken to you."[35]

---

[34] See Songs of Songs 4:16.

[35] John 15:3.

All in attendance should be standing while they listen to the words of the holy Gospel. Each person should have his head uncovered, and should not be leaning on a staff or reclining against any object. They should hear these sacred words with the utmost reverence and awe, for Our Lord proclaimed the divine and highest truth, in clear and undisguised form, in the words of the Gospel.

Hence, those persons who, at any time during the Gospel, genuflect or turn their attention to reciting other prayers are not doing as they should. The Lord Jesus Christ uttered the most sweet and delightful words, speech that was mellifluous, delightful, and eloquent. Indeed, even those who were not disciples of Christ were deeply impressed by the graciousness and power of His words. Hence, we read in the Gospel of John that those who heard His speech exclaimed, "Never has there been a man who spoke as this man speaks!"[36] [And in Luke, we read:] "And they marveled at what He said, for it came from the mouth of God."[37]

Following the reading of the Gospel, something should be said concerning the miraculous and wondrous things that were contained in those holy words, for the benefit of any laity who may be present.[38]

---

[36] John 7:46.

[37] Luke 4:22.

[38] This may have indicated a short homily, or possibly simply a paraphrase of the contents of the Gospel in the vernacular language. Bonaventure's expression *laicis* ("for the laity") suggests it was inserted for the benefit of those who could not understand Latin confidently.

After this follows the recital of the Nicene Creed (*Credo in unum Deum*). For all that Christ preached and which the evangelists recorded in their writings ought to be most firmly believed by the faithful. The Creed, or the expression of the Catholic faith, is called the *symbolum* in Greek. There are three forms of the Creed given to us by the holy fathers. The first one to be formulated was the Apostles' Creed (*Credo in Deum*), which we customarily recite during the celebration of the canonical hours. This form of the Creed, with each of its particular articles, was composed by the most holy apostles of Christ, and reflects the Faith which these same apostles proclaimed courageously throughout the entire world.

But it is to be noted that, in the course of time, various heretics arose, and began to attack and confuse the integrity of the Catholic faith. In response to this, some 318 holy bishops, including Saint Nicholas, held a council at Nicaea in the Year of Our Lord 320. There, they took diligent care to elucidate and clarify the Faith handed on by the apostles. The result was that they produced what is known as the Nicene Creed (*Credo in unum Deum*), and decreed that it should be recited during the Mass. This formulation of the Creed, and the decree for its recitation in the Mass, was strongly approved and confirmed at the Council of Constantinople [in 381] by many holy bishops, amongst whom was Saint Augustine.[39]

---

39 This appears to be an error on the part of Bonaventure, since Saint Augustine is believed to have been converted to the Catholic faith in 386. Some manuscript copies of the work have "Saint Ambrose" here.

The third form of the Creed, which is recited in the celebration of the hour of Prime,[40] and which commences *Quicumque vult*,[41] is believed to have first been issued by Saint Athanasius of Alexandria.

This will suffice for our discussion of the various forms of the Creed.

[40] That is, the Divine Office recited at the first hour of the day (i.e., about 6:00am).

[41] "Whoever wills. . . ." This form of the Creed is known as the Athanasian Creed.

4

THE OFFERTORY UNTIL THE CANON

We will now consider the part of the Mass known as the Offertory. It is called "the Offertory" from the word "offer," because at this point the people bring their offerings to the altar, and thereby display their fidelity and devotion to God. For just as priests are typically joyful when they see many people who are willing to make offerings, so do the apostles rejoice when they witness many people offering themselves to God and accepting the Catholic faith (just as we read in the Acts of the Apostles).

Before the Offertory, the priest will customarily greet the people by saying *Dominus vobiscus* ("The Lord be with you"). He will then summon them to prayer, by saying *Oremus* ("Let us pray"). This is indeed most fitting; for once the words of the holy Gospel have been proclaimed, each mouth should be filled with praise, every action should be rendered fruitful and holy, and all hearts should be confirmed in Faith.

The name "Offertory" also signifies that, in the action which follows, a sacrifice of praise shall be *offered* to the Lord.

The priest, having received the offerings of the people, prepares the chalice with wine and water, and accepts the host from a server. After this, the book containing the Canon of the Mass and the Preface is taken to the left side of the altar, close to where the Gospel is customarily read. It is to be noted that the right corner of the altar signifies the Jewish people, and the left corner signifies the Gentiles. The movement of the missal to the left side represents that fact that the Gentiles first received their faith in God through the Jewish people. And if only one candle is to be used on the altar, it is placed on the left side. This signifies that we, who celebrate the liturgy, are descendants of the Gentile races.

Once this has been done, the paten and the chalice are made ready. Wine and water are commingled in the chalice; and the bread and wine to be consecrated are both elevated above the altar.

The quadrilateral form of altar signifies the cross, with its four corners. The chalice represents the tomb of Our Lord, and the pall placed upon it is a figure of the stone positioned over the entrance of this tomb. The corporal signifies the clean white sheet that was placed over the dead Body of Christ.

The roundness of the Host symbolizes the eternity of the Triune God. For a circular form (that is, one which has the quality of roundness) has neither a beginning nor an end. The divine eternity likewise is without beginning, and shall certainly never come to an end. This eternity of the Divinity had already been declared at the conclusion of the Collect, which always finishes with *per omnia sæcula.*[42]

The altar, when it is consecrated by a bishop, is anointed on each of its four corners, reflecting symbolically and venerating the form of the cross. Indeed, the whole Catholic Church has been similarly anointed with the Blood of Christ. Hence it is that in a famous Passiontide hymn, we sing: *De crucis stipite, quem sacer cruor perunxit* ("Of the branch of cross, which the sacred Blood anointed").[43]

The altar is likewise covered with a clean, white cloth, just as the cross itself was adorned by the pure and spotless humanity of Christ, which hung therefrom. And in the altar, various relics of the saints are concealed, just as in the cross the greatest and most holy mysteries are hidden—namely, the length, breadth, height and depth of God's love!

We shall now speak of the mixing of the water and wine in the chalice. Only a small quantity of water should be mixed with the wine, so that the water is completely absorbed within the wine. If anyone (may it never happen!) should mix in a very large quantity of water, such that it negates or overpowers the quality and flavor of the wine, then the priest does not validly consecrate the Blood of Christ, and commits a serious act of

---

42 'Through all ages' (i.e., 'forever and ever').

43 This line is from the Passiontide hymn *Pange lingua gloriosi* by Venantius Fortunatus (530–610).

negligence. The water, indeed, signifies humanity, and the wine represents divinity. When the water is mixed with the wine, the humanity and the people are united with Christ. Hence great care is to be taken that the adding of the water should not be omitted, lest the people of God be separated from Christ.

The host is positioned next to the chalice because Christ (symbolized by the host) offered Himself for the Church (symbolized by the chalice). The host is formed from many grains of wheat being brought together in one substance, and similarly, the wine is created from the mixture of the juice of many grapes. Through this, we may understand that Christ is united with the many members of the Church through the waters of Baptism, who together form a single Body. Hence, the Apostle (St. Paul) writes, "And the two shall be as one body. This is a great sacrament, I say—both in Christ and in the Church."[44]

In the celebration of the principal feast days, the chalice and host, together with the altar, are incensed. This signifies that the faithful people, together with the priest, ought to offer holy prayers, both individually and collectively. On solemnities, the priest customarily uses different and proper Collects, Prefaces, and *Communicantes* in the Canon of the Mass.[45] Thus, both he and the people assembled together offer special prayers to God and His saints. It is of such prayers that the

---

44 Ephesians 5:31–32.

45 This refers to the section of the Roman Canon commencing with the word *Communicantes* ("In communion with. . .").

psalmist, speaking in the person of the Church, says: *Dirigatur oratio mea sicut incensum.*[46]

Then, the chalice having been prepared and the offerings and altar having been incensed, the priest then customarily bows profoundly in prayer. After this, he turns toward the people and silently requests that they should pray for him. We shall briefly explain what this signifies. In the Gospels, we read that many were converted by the preaching of Christ, to the extent that the Pharisees exclaimed, "Behold, the whole world is going after Him!"[47] And, because of Christ raising Lazarus from the dead, the envious Pharisees held a council to plan how they could kill not only Our Lord, but the risen Lazarus as well.[48] But because His hour had not yet come for Him to undergo death, He hid Himself until Palm Sunday, and dedicated Himself to secret prayer and teaching His inner circle of apostles. And this is what is signified by the silence and the profound bow of the priest after the offertory. And again, after Palm Sunday until Good Friday, Christ urged His disciples to pray that they should not be led into temptation. This is represented by the priest turning toward the people, and silently requesting their prayer. This takes place just before the *Secretum* [or Prayer over the Gifts].

---

46 "May my prayer be directed as incense." Psalm 140:2.

47 John 12:19.

48 John 12:10–11.

The *Secretum* [which is traditionally said inaudibly] represents the unseen prayer of Christ in the garden of Gethsemane, in which His sweat fell like great drops of blood.

Again, when Our Lord told the Jews that they had killed all the prophets sent to them and they spurned His words, He said to them, "I say to you, you shall not see Me anymore now, until you say, 'Blessed is He Who comes in the name of the Lord!'"[49] And then He concealed Himself from their sight until the time determined by the Father. And, according to this divine determination, He showed Himself again on Palm Sunday, presenting Himself humbly as an offering riding on a donkey. And then what He had prophesied was fulfilled, for "the children of the Hebrews, together with the great crowd who had gathered for the Passover feast, cried out, saying: 'Blessed is He Who comes in the name of the Lord! Hosanna in the highest!'"[50] All of this is figured in the Mass by the actions of the priest, from the *Secretum* until the *Sanctus,* in which the verse "Blessed is He Who comes in the name of the Lord" is proclaimed.

It must be recognized that the *Preface* possesses an importance and significance that should not be overlooked or underestimated. The Church, still fighting here on earth, here implores that her voice may be united with the blessed spirits and angelic virtues in heaven. And this will indeed take place if, according to the exhortation of the priests, we have "lifted

[49] Matthew 23:39.

[50] Cf. Matthew 21:9.

up our hearts to the Lord," and thus separated them from all earthly desires and distractions.

For there can be no doubt that in the Mass, the highest celestial spirits are united with our lowliness. For Scripture states that "where the body is [that is, where the Mass is celebrated], there the eagles [that is, the holy angels] shall gather."[51] We pray *three* times that our voice may become *one* with those of the holy angels, by singing three times the word *Sanctus.* In this manner, we signify that God is both three [in persons] and one [in divine substance].

Moreover, by singing *Sanctus* three times, we affirm that the Lord is supreme in the three realms—that is, in the heavens, on earth, and in the underworld, so that every knee shall bend at the holy name of Jesus in each of these realms.[52] By singing this threefold *Sanctus* it is as if we proclaim:

> Almighty God,
> You are holy, protecting Your faithful upon this earth;
> You are holy, filling all the saints and angels in heaven with indescribable joy;
> [You are holy, freeing the souls in the underworld from the bonds of death].[53]

---

[51] Matthew 24:28. This passage is often translated differently from the Vulgate text, which Bonaventure cites here.

[52] See Philippians 2:10.

[53] This last acclamation is not in the original text. However, it seems to be necessary to complete the threefold repetition of the *Sanctus* and corresponds with the three realms (heaven, earth, and the underworld) referred to by Bonaventure a little earlier.

To the triple acclamation of the holiness of God, the word *Sabaoth* is added. This means "of hosts" or "of armies." "Blessed," therefore, "is He Who comes in the name of the Lord"—that is, in the name of God the Father—and deigned for our salvation to assume human flesh and undergo for our sake the torments of the Cross!

The phrase *Hosanna in excelsis* is sung during the *Sanctus.* "Hosanna" is interpreted as "save." Hence, the Church implores, "O Christ, You Who are powerful on high, save us who struggle upon the earth!" This line, *Hosanna in excelsis*, is sung twice during this chant, thereby indicating the twofold glory and sanctity of the saints in heaven—that is to say, the glory and sanctity both of the soul and of the body.

It is also pertinent to note that the text of the Mass includes three different and venerable sacred languages, namely Hebrew, Greek, and Latin. Through this is fulfilled what is written in the Scriptures, "Every tongue shall confess that Jesus Christ is Lord, in the glory of God the Father."[54] Hebrew words in the Mass include *Sabaoth, Hosanna, Amen*, and *Alleluia.* Greek words are to be found in the *Kyrie eleison.* And the Epistle and Gospel, etc. are all spoken in Latin. The use of these three sacred languages represents and reflects the inscription that was placed upon the cross, "Jesus the Nazarene, the King of the Jews," which was written in the same three languages—namely, Greek, Hebrew and Latin.[55]

---

54 Philippians 2:11.

55 See John 19:20.

Before the commencement of the Canon of the Mass, the priest washes his fingers. This action expresses that only those who have been washed from the dominion of sin through Baptism ought to be present for the consecration of the Body of Christ, which will very shortly occur.[56]

[56] At the time when Bonaventure was writing, the non-baptized were not permitted to be present during the Consecration. Of course, infant baptism was the universal practice in Europe throughout the Middle Ages.

5

THE CANON OF THE MASS: PART I

We should now consider the Canon of the Mass itself.[57] This great Eucharistic Prayer was composed by various saints. But a certain scholar of the Roman Church, at the request of the Apostolic See [then occupied by Pope Saint Gregory the Great], placed it in its definitive order.[58]

The most holy and potent utterances [the words of consecration] were placed, by the will of Christ Himself, in the central place in the text of the Canon. This corresponds to the positioning of the heart—the organ which gives and sustains life—in the central position within the human body. The most sacred words of consecration, by which the priest makes present

57 The Canon of the Mass, also known as the Roman Canon, corresponds closely with what is referred to as Eucharistic Prayer I in the *Novus Ordo* Missal.

58 The word used here is *scholasticus*. This means "scholar," but could also have been the name of a person, and is sometimes interpreted as such. Medieval manuscripts are generally very inconsistent in the use of capitals for proper nouns.

the very Body and Blood of Christ, are found in the middle of the Canon, like a divine King positioned in the center of a great army or court.

Many of the saints have composed and added passages to the text of the Canon, including Popes Gelasius [I], Damasus [I], Gregory [the Great], Leo [the Great], and Sergius [I].[59] But there are also other saints who have contributed to its formation. In the time of the apostles themselves, the Eucharistic Prayer consisted only of the text [of the consecration], commencing from "*Qui pridie.* . . ."[60] Then would follow the text of the consecration, with the Lord's Prayer after that.

The Canon itself should be spoken in a well-judged manner, and in an undertone.[61] The speaking of the words in a well-judged manner is important. Accordingly, they should not be leapt over with excessive speed. On the other hand, they must not be unduly protracted, as this gives rise to tedium in those who are present. The Church has decreed that the words of the Canon should be spoken in an undertone, or *sotto voce.* For this quietness portrays the humility of Christ. For, when He was in the presence of His accusers and judge, He offered

---

59 These popes are not listed by Bonaventure in chronological order. Possibly, Bonaventure named them in order of the relative magnitude of their contributions to the text of the Roman Canon.

60 "Who, on the day before [He suffered]. . . ."

61 Although the term used here is "*sub silentio*," it was assumed, the words were truly spoken, and still audible to the priest himself. The translation given ("in an undertone") seems to reflect this best.

no reply, and "as a Lamb about to be shorn, He opened not His mouth."[62]

The beginning of the Canon of the Mass is *Te, igitur, clementissime Pater. . . .*[63] It is to be noted that this conjunction, *igitur* ("therefore"), refers to the Preface and the *Sanctus,* which is sung immediately before the Canon. Here it is as if the priest says, in the person of the Church, "Almighty God, since You have heard and accepted our song of praise, which we have sung to Your glory in union with the holy angels, *therefore,* most merciful Father, we humbly pray and beseech You (through Jesus Christ), that You accept and bless these gifts. . . ."

It is to be noticed that Divine Providence has wisely decreed that the first letter of the Canon of the Mass should be a *T* (*Te, igitur. . .*). This capital letter *T* shows to us very clearly the holy sign of the cross. In many sacramentaries (that is, the books containing the Canon of the Mass), an illustrated image of a crucifix is used to illuminate this initial letter. In this way, not only the form of the letter *T* but its visual elaboration serves as a timely reminder of the passion of Our Lord. For the letter *T* signifies the mystery of the cross, as the Lord declares through the prophet [Ezekiel], "Inscribe a *T* upon the foreheads of those who mourn and weep, lest they are struck by My angel."[64] And, indeed, a cross is inscribed upon our foreheads through the anointing of Confirmation, so that we receive thereby the

---

62 Isaiah 53:7.

63 "To You, therefore, most merciful Father. . . ."

64 Ezekiel 9:4.

anointing of the Lord's most holy passion, and our minds are inflamed with devotion to this mystery.

The relationship of the passion of the Lord to the sacrifice of the Mass is of such paramount importance that the holy fathers decreed that no priest should ever celebrate the Eucharist unless an image of the crucified Savior be present and visible. And the priest, upon beholding this sacred image, and seeing the loving arms of Jesus extended upon the cross, should join with Him in extending his own arms in prayer (in the manner of a cross), to supplicate the Lord for the sins of the people. Through this, the words of Paul are fulfilled: "Far be it from me to glory except in the cross!"[65]

Because we have made mention of the cross, or elements which signify the cross, it is fitting that here we should say a little about this wondrous mystery. The cross was the "dominion laid upon the shoulders" of Our Savior.[66] O marvelous and incomparable sign, and pledge replete with all spiritual fruitfulness! The cross is that Tree of Life located in the middle of the garden of Paradise, which the four rivers of the Gospel irrigate. The cross is pure love, in which was perfected the true ark of salvation, which is the holy Church. The cross is the altar upon which Abraham offered his son Isaac as a sacrifice—or rather, the altar upon which the Father of the heavens sacrificed Our Lord Jesus Christ. The cross is the wood which was cast into the

---

[65] Galatians 6:14.

[66] Isaiah 9:6.

bitter waters at Mara, and rendered them sweet;[67] and which was cast into the bitter waters of this world, and rendered the harsh rigidity and austerity of the old law delightful and sweet by the new law of love. For the old law had taught, "You must hate your enemy," and "An eye for an eye, and a tooth for a tooth." Yet the new law of love replaces these bitter and harsh precepts with the sweetness of charity, compassion, and mercy.

The cross is the rod with which the true rock (that is, Christ) was struck, and which caused to flow forth the abundant streams of blood and water.[68] In these mystical streams, our souls are cleansed of their impurities and given everlasting salvation. The cross is that staff on which the bronze serpent (that is, Christ) was raised up.[69] And all who behold this new serpent with the eyes of faith are healed of the venom of the bite of the ancient, fiery serpent (the devil). The cross is the lyre upon which our true David (that is, Christ), graciously played, and thereby dispelled the power of the evil spirits from Saul (that is, from the human race). The cross is the key of David,[70] which opens wide the portals to the kingdom of heaven that we may enter therein.

The priest makes three signs of the cross over the chalice at the beginning of the Canon. What this threefold repetition of this holy sign signifies we shall now explain. These signify

---

67 See Exodus 15: 22–25.

68 See Numbers 20:6–11.

69 See Numbers 21:6–9; John 3:14–15.

70 Revelation 3:7.

the three "handings-over" by which Our Lord was given up to death. Firstly, the Son was handed over to the world by God the Father, as is expressed by the Apostle [St. Paul], "He did not spare His only Son, but for all of our sakes handed Him over."[71] This first "Handing-over" is signified by the first sign of the cross over the chalice, when the words *hæc dona* ("these gifts") are pronounced. The second "Handing-over" was when the Son freely gave Himself up to death. Of this, the prophet Isaiah writes, "He gave up His soul to death, and was numbered amongst the guilty."[72] This second "Handing-over" is represented by the second sign of the cross made over the chalice, which occurs when the words *hæc munera* ("these offerings") are spoken. And God graciously and lovingly accepted this noble self-offering of His only begotten Son.

The third "Handing-over" of Christ to death was that done by the traitor, Judas. Of this treacherous betrayal, Matthew writes, "The one who handed Him over gave to them a sign, saying, 'The one Whom I shall kiss. . . .'"[73] This third and wicked "handing-over" is signified by the third sign of the cross made over the chalice. This third sign of the cross coincides with the words *sacrificia illibata* ("this unblemished Sacrifice"). The description *illibata* [which means both "unblemished" and "unsacrificed"] pertains [in the sense of "unsacrificed"] to the bread and wine, which have not previously been offered as a

71 Romans 8:32.

72 Isaiah 53:12.

73 Matthew 26:48.

sacrifice. [But, in the sense of "unblemished,"] it pertains to Christ Himself.[74] For Christ was indeed entirely free from the blemish of sin. He was born without sin and lived without sin, and died as one wholly innocent. Therefore, His death was holy and unblemished. This word "unblemished" reflects the perfect innocence of Christ, Who was pure from all stain of iniquity, as the Apostle [Saint Peter] declares, "He committed no sin."[75]

---

[74] The original text has been slightly paraphrased here, to clarify Bonaventure's explanation of the twofold meaning of *illibata.*

[75] 1 Peter 2:22.

6

THE CANON OF THE MASS: PART II

Proceeding onwards with the Canon of the Mass, next follows the text, "Which we offer You firstly for Your holy Catholic Church." It is indeed very useful and appropriate to pray for our holy Mother, the Church. For whoever prays sincerely for the Church becomes a sharer and participant in all her merits, good actions, and blessings. The priest prays together with all those present, asking that he may be heard by the Father through Jesus—that is, on account of Jesus Christ, His Son. It is as if he is praying thus: "If we do not deserve to be heard because of our many sins, at least deign to hear us, O God, on account of Your only begotten Son, that You may bestow peace upon Your Church and guard and protect her from all peril. For unless You protect us, O Lord, 'in vain does the watchman keep guard.'[76] And may You deign also to *unite* the Church, for 'any kingdom which is divided shall be left

[76] Psalm 126:1.

desolate.'[77] And if You do not *govern* Your Church, she shall surely be torn apart by schism."

Next follows a prayer for the Roman Pontiff, expressed in the words, "together with Your servant, our Pope." It is to be noted that this memorial of the Apostolic See is included in all Masses, as decreed in various councils. But the priest should never include the personal name of the pope in saying the prayer [but identify him simply as "our Pope,"] and call his name to mind in his memory only.[78]

Next we pray for *antistite nostro*—that is, "our bishop." Then we pray for our king. This is to be understood as referring to the King of the Romans, or the Holy Roman Emperor. Again, the personal name of the monarch should never be mentioned.[79] In this series of prayers, we can see how the priest is bound to supplicate faithfully before God on behalf of the Church, and for those who exercise spiritual and temporal power in the world.

Next, he prays for "all those who, holding to the truth, hand on the Catholic, apostolic and orthodox faith." This phrase may be understood as encompassing all cardinals, primates, patriarchs, archbishops, bishops, prelates, and priests, as well

---

77 Luke 11:17.

78 This practice undoubtedly reflects the fact that during the Middle Ages, there were very frequent rival contenders to the papacy (or anti-popes), and so there was often genuine uncertainty about who was the legitimate pope. Moreover, there were many periods when the papal see was vacant.

79 Again, this reflects the fact that there were often rival claimants to the imperial crown during the Middle Ages.

as all those who support them in their work. Each Mass is to include a prayer for persons entrusted with these sacred ministries.

Next follows, "Remember, O Lord, Your servants. . . ." At this point, the priest offers prayers for all those who have presented him with any benefits. To this he adds, "and all here present." Thus the priest offers supplication for all in attendance and commends them faithfully to God. It is as if he is saying, "O God, *You* know the faith and devotion of those assembled here much better than I do! Therefore, correct in them whatever You may find to be in need of correction, and help them as they need to be helped."

The text which follows is: "who offer to You"—that is, "the eternal God, living and true"—a sacrifice of praise "for themselves and all who are dear to them." Note that we refer to the Father of Our Lord Jesus Christ, together with [Christ Himself and] the Holy Spirit, as "the eternal God, living and true." This is to distinguish the God we worship from the false gods who are *not* living and *not* true—that is to say, from all the idols to which the heathens make sacrifice. It is of these that the psalmist writes, "The idols of the pagans are silver and gold, the work of human hands." And again, "they have mouths but do not speak," precisely because they are not living. And if such idols "have ears but do not hear," can they be expected to hear the prayers of their misguided suppliants?[80] Surely not!

80 Psalm 113B:4–6.

Next follows the text commencing with *Communicantes,* or "In communion with. . . ." This reflects that the sacrifice of the Mass is always and only offered in communion with the Church, and may never be offered outside of that communion. It is therefore offered in union with the whole Church [both on earth and in heaven], including the whole communion of the saints. It is as if the Church Militant, or the Church still struggling here on earth, says, "Even if, on account of our many sins and failings, *we* do not merit to be heard, nevertheless, through our communion with the assembly of the saints, including the Blessed Virgin Mary and the glorious apostles and martyrs, let our prayers be graciously received by You, O Lord! We invoke their aid, and You, O Lord, will surely not refuse to listen to them. Because *they* are worthy to be heard, You shall also certainly deign to listen to our own humble prayers and petitions, which are offered to You in union with them."

We should explain why there is not a specific mention of the saints who are *confessors,* whereas there is a specific mention of the martyrs. There are two reasons for this. The word "martyr" is of Greek origin, and means, literally, "a witness." The martyrs are mentioned in the Roman Canon because they are witnesses through their own holy death to the passion of Christ [which is what is represented in the sacrifice of the Mass]. The second reason is that this part of the Canon was written either by Pope Gelasius [I],[81] or a certain Roman scholastic [who was engaged

81 Died 496.

by Pope Gregory the Great]. Now, it was only somewhat later that feasts celebrating confessors began to be celebrated. [At that time, only martyrs had feast days.]

So, the priest is able to offer the Mass in honor of a saint who is a confessor, but he does not explicitly mention such a saint in the recitation of the Canon. But the priest does add [to the names of the martyrs], "and all Your saints," thus including the entire communion of holy souls.

It is to be noted that the Blessed Virgin Mary, because she is exalted far above all saints and angels, is always mentioned first in the Canon.

Following this affirmation of our communion with all the saints, the prayer continues with the words, "through whose merits" [i.e., making intercession through the merits of the saints]. In a similar way did Moses pray, when he said, "Remember, O Lord, Abraham, Isaac, and Jacob, to whom You swore a covenant. . . ."[82] In calling to mind the merits of the saints to offer his prayer, it is as if the priest is saying, "Lord, You shall surely listen to me more readily, as I make remembrance of the merits of Your beloved saints."

See, O Reader, how in the Mass that which is lowly is constantly united to that which is exalted! Earthly things are transformed into celestial realities, and the struggling Church on earth is brought into unity with the glorious and triumphant

[82] Exodus 32:13.

Church in heaven! And this is both brought about and expressed through the Canon of the Mass.

Next follows the petition, "Therefore, Lord, we pray: graciously accept this oblation of our service, that of Your whole family; order our days in Your peace, and command that we be delivered from eternal damnation and counted among the flock of those You have chosen." These words were added to the Canon by Pope Saint Gregory the Great.[83] Indeed, their meaning and the sentiment they express are beautifully clear and lucid; so no further explanation of them is necessary.

---

83 Died 604.

7

THE CANON OF THE MASS: PART III

The text which follows petitions the Lord that the consecration which shall soon occur may be efficacious in making present the true Body and Blood of Our Savior. It reads thus:

Quam oblationem tu, Deus, in omnibus, quæsumus,
benedictam,† adscriptam,† ratam,†
rationabilem, acceptabilemque facere digneris:
ut nobis Corpus† et Sanguis† fiat dilectissimi Filii tui Domini nostri Jesu Christi.

["We beseech You, O God, that in all respects You may deign to make this oblation blessed, † adscriptam,† ratam,[84]† reasonable, and acceptable:

[84] It is difficult to find perfectly satisfactory English translations for these two Latin words. In his exposition which follows, Bonaventure treats the words "*adscriptam*" and "*ratam*" quite literally (meaning, respectively, "having been written about," and "highly regarded" or "recognized"). But they also carry the senses, respectively, of "acknowledged" and "approved."

That it may become for us the Body† and Blood† of Your most beloved Son, Our Lord Jesus Christ."]

We should consider why the sign of the cross is made five times over the Host and chalice during the utterance of these words. Firstly, the diversity and multiplicity of signs made during the Canon represent the many and diverse forms of torments and sufferings to which Christ was subject during His most holy passion. The five signs of the cross during these particular words symbolize the fact that each of the five senses of Our Lord were tormented during His passion. He suffered in each of His five senses so that He might bring light and illumination to each of our five senses, which had hitherto been darkened by sin.

Firstly, Christ suffered in His *vision,* when He was blindfolded by the soldiers and thus deprived of sight. He suffered in His *hearing,* when He heard the words of mockery and derision. He was tormented also in His sense of *taste,* when He was given gall and vinegar to drink. He was afflicted through His sense of *smell,* by the foul stench at Calvary, which was polluted by the rotting corpses of criminals and malefactors. And most terribly did He suffer through His sense of *touch,* when the sharp nails were cruelly driven into His flesh.

Another meaning contained in the five signs of the cross made during the words quoted above is this. Three of them [those which are said to coincide with the words *benedictam, adscriptam*, and *ratam*] symbolize the three classes of people to whom Jesus was betrayed by Judas—namely, the priests, scribes, and Pharisees. But the text of the Canon refutes each of these classes in turn: firstly, by asserting (to the priests of the Temple) that Jesus was *blessed,* since He was the "blessed fruit of the womb" of Mary; secondly, by affirming (to the scribes) that He was *adscriptam,* that is to say, the prophets had written of His coming in the Sacred Scriptures; and thirdly, by pointing out (to the Pharisees) that He is *ratam,* or recognized and approved, for His kingdom shall endure without end.

There remain two crosses apart from these three, and these are the two which are made specially over the Host and the chalice separately [coinciding with the words "Body" and "Blood" respectively]. These two crosses signify the fact that the traitor, Judas, who failed to return to his faith through true repentance for his treachery, was condemned in a twofold way—that is, in both body and soul.

In this text, it is prayed that God shall make this oblation "rational" and "acceptable." Here it is as if the priest is saying, "In the Old Testament a sacrifice was offered which was entirely *irrational,* since it consisted only of unthinking animals and other things lacking the faculty of reason. But, in contrast to this ancient sacrifice, may You, most holy and merciful Father, make our sacrifice completely *rational.* And may You also make it *acceptable,* so that it may render us acceptable to You, O Lord. May the bread which is now positioned upon the altar become the Body which confers life to our own bodies, so that we may partake of eternal life and escape the dominion of death. And may the wine which is in this chalice become the Blood which sanctifies our souls, so that we may be free from unending condemnation. And this life-giving Body and Blood which is able to save us is the Body and Blood of Your beloved Son, Our Lord Jesus Christ!"

8

THE CANON OF THE MASS: PART IV

The Words of Consecration and the Elevation

The Canon of the Mass continues with the words, "On the day before He suffered" (that is, on the day before Good Friday) "He took bread in His holy and venerable hands. . . ," and what follows, including the most holy words of consecration. These sacred words are given in full below:

Qui pridie quam pateretur, accepit
panem in sanctas, ac venerabiles
manus suas, et elevatis oculis in
cælum ad te Deum Patrem suum
omnipotentem, tibi gratias agens,
benedixit, fregit, deditque discipulis
suis, dicens:
Accipite, et manducate ex hoc omnes.
HOC EST ENIM CORPUS MEUM.

Simili modo postquam cœnatum est,
accipiens et hunc præclarum Calicem
in sanctas ac venerabiles manus suas:
item tibi gratias agens, benedixit,
deditque discipulis suis, dicens:
Accipite, et bibite ex eo omnes.
HIC EST ENIM CALIX SANGUINIS
MEI, NOVI ET ÆTERNI
TESTAMENTI: MYSTERIUM FIDEI:
QUI PRO VOBIS ET PRO MULTIS
EFFUNDETUR IN REMISSIONEM
PECCATORUM.
Hæc quotiescumque feceritis, in mei
memoriam facietis.

["Who, the day before He suffered,
took bread into His holy and venerable
hands, and with His eyes raised to
heaven, unto You, God, His almighty
Father, giving thanks to You, He
blessed it, broke it, and gave it to His
disciples saying:
Take, all of you, and eat of this.
FOR THIS IS MY BODY.
In like manner, after He had supped,
taking also this excellent chalice into
His holy and venerable hands, and again
giving thanks to You, He blessed it,
and gave it to His disciples, saying:

> Take, all of you, and drink of this:
> FOR THIS IS THE CHALICE OF MY
> BLOOD OF THE NEW AND ETERNAL
> TESTAMENT: THE MYSTERY OF
> FAITH: WHICH SHALL BE POURED
> OUT FOR YOU AND FOR MANY
> UNTO THE REMISSION OF SINS.
> As often as you shall do these things,
> you do them in memory of Me."]

In these words, the Holy Trinity, together with the priest, truly blesses the bread and wine—by a miraculous, hidden, and ineffable blessing—thus changing (*mutando*) them into the true Body and Blood of Christ. This happens as the phrases *Hoc est enim corpus meum,*[85] and *Hic est calix sanguinis mei*[86] are pronounced.

It is to be noted that the priest holds his hands extended, toward both corners of the altar. In this way, he physically forms the image of a cross, representing the crucified Christ and calling to mind the sacrifice of His passion.[87] The fact that his hands are extended toward both sides of the altar (which represent the Jewish and Gentile peoples, respectively, as has been previously noted) expresses the fact that Christ died for both

---

85 "This is indeed My Body."

86 "This is the chalice of My Blood."

87 This gesture is not included in the Tridentine Roman rite but is found in the current rites of the Dominicans, Carthusians, and Carmelites. Clearly, it was the practice among Franciscans also when Bonaventure was writing.

these peoples—that is to say, for all humanity. For He came to lead the Jewish people back to the way of righteousness and truth, and to establish the Catholic faith among the Gentiles.

It now behooves us to consider why it is that the priest elevates the Body of Christ above the altar, so that it is visible to all who are present. Indeed, there are many mystical reasons why the most holy Body of Our Lord is elevated during the Mass.

The very first of these is to obtain the grace of God the Father, which through our sins and iniquities we lose. By sin alone is God offended and angered, as is expressed by the psalmist: "They angered God by their doings."[88] The priest therefore elevates the Body of Christ to God the Father, as if saying, "O heavenly Father, we have sinned and thereby provoked You to wrath. But now look upon the face of Your Christ, which we now offer to You in order to turn You away from Your anger, toward mercy instead. Turn not Your face from Your Child—that is, Your only begotten Son—and remember those words You once spoke to Him, 'This is My beloved Son, in Whom I am well pleased.'[89] Therefore, O Lord, correct in us mercifully whatever You find in need of correction. Turn us to Yourself, and avert Your wrath away from us!"[90]

The second cause of the elevation of the Host is to implore and obtain those good things which are necessary for us during this present life. The first good thing which we are in need of

---

88 Psalm 105:29.

89 Matthew 3:17.

90 Cf. Psalm 84:5.

in this mortal life is *peace* [that is to say, reconciliation] for our sins, which no one is able to obtain unless he has been freed from his mortal sins by the grace of God. This reconciliation is the peace of which Christ spoke when He said, "My peace I give to you."[91] The second good thing of which we stand in need is *charity*, for this virtue causes us to flourish in both the present and the future life. For charity properly directs each person's life in this present world in such a manner that it shall lead to the attainment of the glory of the future, eternal life. Hence it is that the apostle Saint John declares that "He who remains in charity, remains in God."[92] Therefore, when the priest elevates the Host, it is as if he is announcing to all those present, "If you wish to obtain that which your hearts most truly desire, then seek to maintain mutual charity. For Christ, through His death, has reconciled us to God and the angelic host; and, through the virtue of charity, has opened to us access to joys which endure forever."

The third reason for the elevation of the Body of Christ is to remind us of that which is our right and our inheritance; which we already possess in our hearts in firm *hope*, and shall possess in the future in concrete *reality* in the heavenly kingdom. This inheritance that we shall receive in heaven is nothing other than life eternal. Hence it is that John, in his Gospel, records the words of Christ, Who said, "I have come into the

---

[91] John 14:27.

[92] 1 John 4:16.

world, so that they" [that is, those who imitate Him] "may have life" [that is, may have life in this present world] "and have it more abundantly"[93] [that is, so that they may possess eternal life in the world to come]. This glorious inheritance of ours has been faithfully recorded and indelibly inscribed with a pen of iron—that is to say, with the lance which pierced the side of Our Savior, and the nails which were driven through His hands and feet. Hence it is that when the priest elevates the Body of Christ over the altar, it is as if he proclaims, "O you angelic spirits, who are here present among us, you are witnesses of the lawful inheritance which has been promised to us, which is eternal life. And to confirm and testify to this, we hold aloft the pledge which has been given to us, which is the Body of Christ, Who for our sakes did suffer and die!"

The fourth reason for the elevation of the Body of Christ at this point is to display the *power* of God. Great indeed is the power of God, for by the mere pronouncement of the words, "This is My Body," He is able to transubstantiate common bread into His true flesh! This is what is referred to in the psalm as the "mutation of the right hand of the Most High,"[94] and entirely transcends our human comprehension. Thus when the priest elevates the Body of Christ, it is as if he is saying, "Just before, you perceived mere bread upon the altar, but now that the words of consecration have been uttered, behold, here is

---

93 John 10:10.

94 Psalm 76:11.

the true Body of Christ! And if God is able to bring about such a wondrous transformation in this bread, He is certainly able to transform our sins and faults into grace, and finally into eternal glory!"

The fifth reason why the Body of Christ is elevated is to declare and exhibit the astounding *wisdom* of God. With wondrous wisdom, which surpasses all words, Christ displays Himself to us in a hidden form. Of this hidden form, the prophet Isaiah says, "Truly, You are a God Who is hidden, O God of Israel, Our Savior!"[95]

It should be recognized that there are many reasons why Our Lord and God, Jesus Christ, chooses to conceal Himself in the form of bread. For if He was to appear on the altar as He really is [in His divine glory], or if He were to exhibit His Body as it was on the cross, many would surely be too terrified to consume the most holy Body of Christ. Indeed, some would certainly rush away in fear and confusion, as is expressed in the Gospel: "Many [indeed, even the disciples] when they heard the words, 'Unless you eat of the flesh of the Son of Man,' departed, and no longer walked with Him."[96] Those who heard these words thought that they were being directed to cut up His members, and thus to consume His flesh. And this is unquestionably something which is repulsive and horrible to our human sensibilities. Rather, it was Christ's intention to veil His

---

[95] Isaiah 45:15.

[96] John 6:54, 67.

Body and Blood under the appearances of bread and wine, and thereby to give these to the faithful to consume in an acceptable manner.

There are other reasons, also, why Our Lord chooses to conceal His Flesh and Blood under the appearances of the sacramental forms of bread and wine. But we shall pass over these other reasons for the moment.

The sixth reason for the elevation of the Body of Christ above the altar is to manifest His infinite *generosity*. For what generosity is greater than this: that God has given unto human beings the very bread of angels to eat? Thus, when the priest elevates the Body of Christ above the altar, it is as if he proclaims, "O faithful of Christ, look and rejoice! This is indeed the celestial banquet of the angels, which the most generous King of heaven has bestowed upon us so that we may be filled with all grace and blessing!" And reference to this generous gift and its effect is made a little later in the text of the Canon, when the priest prays that "all of us, who through this participation at the altar, receive the most holy Body and Blood of Your Son may be filled with every grace and heavenly blessing."

But woe to those who disdain to receive the Body of the Lord, truly present in this heavenly banquet! For such persons make themselves strangers to Christ. It was of such persons that Elisha speaks, when (as recorded in the book of Kings) he says, "You shall see, but will not taste!"[97] Alas, how many there

[97] 2 (4) Kings 7:2.

are who see the Body of Christ, but do not taste it! For, through their deplorable state of mortal sin, they have alienated themselves from the Body of the Lord.

The seventh reason why the Body of Christ is elevated above the altar is to show the *goodness* of Christ. What greater goodness could there possibly be, than that Our Lord has deigned to be truly present upon the altar, and to be held as if He is a captive victim for sacrifice? It is of this which He speaks through the prophet Jeremiah, where it is written, "Behold, I am in your hands! Do unto me whatever is good and right in your eyes."[98] Note that whenever any illustrious and noble leader is captured and held as a hostage, he is not released until a large ransom has been paid. In a similar way, Christ (Who has consented to become a hostage for our sake) is not released until He has granted to us forgiveness for our sins and admission into the kingdom of heaven. Therefore, when the priest raises the Body of Christ, our captive Victim, above the altar, it is as if he declares, "Behold, the One Whom the whole universe is not able to contain, is now held as a captive Victim on this altar! And we shall not release Him until He grants to us the ransom we desire—namely, the forgiveness of our sins and admission into the kingdom of heaven!"

The eighth reason for the elevation of the precious Body of Christ above the altar is to impart *joy* to the entire holy Catholic Church, through the raising of this sacred Host, which is

---

98 Jeremiah 26:14.

indeed for us the flag of exultant triumph and glorious victory. All of us, who fight and struggle under this splendid flag, receive from the sight of it fortitude and joy. Each member of the Church is destined and called to fight as a soldier during this life; and hence it is that holy Job once wrote, "The life of man is a term of military service."[99] Thus when the priest elevates the Body of Christ above the altar, it is as if he is exhorting all members of the Church, "Do not fear, but fight with courage! Behold, this is our flag, which, for our sake, was raised up high upon the cross, and tinctured red with the Blood of the passion. Behold, this is Our Lord and Commander, Jesus Christ, now here present amongst us!"

The final and ninth reason for the priest elevating the Body of Christ above the altar is to imitate and follow the example of Christ Himself. It was so that sinners may be encouraged to repent and not fall into despair that Christ revealed His wounded Body. He showed to God the Father the wound upon His side, and the cruel scars left upon His hands and feet, and these very wounds act as advocates for His mercy, and plead for our cause. Accordingly, Saint Bernard once wrote, "We have secure and safe access to God, for the Son shows His wounds to the Father on our behalf to beseech His mercy for us." When the priest raises the sacred Body of Christ on high, it is as if he proclaims to sinners and to all Christians, "Behold, the Son of God, Who for us was stretched out and raised up upon the

---

[99] Job 7:1.

altar of the cross! Follow Him, and be willing to suffer for Him at least a little, since He suffered for us so very, very much!" This is in accordance with the words of the apostle Saint Peter, who reminds us that "Christ suffered for us."[100] Therefore, we, in turn, should be prepared to share in His sufferings, so that we may ever be mindful of the benefits of His passion and filled with hope for the glory of His resurrection.

[100] 1 Peter 2:21.

9

THE CANON OF THE MASS: PART V

After the words of consecration, next follows the prayer of devotion:

Unde et memores, Domine, nos servi tui, sed et plebs tua sancta,
ejusdem Christi Filii tui, Domini nostri,
tam beatæ passionis,
nec non et ab inferis resurrectionis,
sed et in cælos gloriosæ ascensionis:
offerimus præclaræ majestati tuæ de tuis donis ac datis
hostiam† puram,
hostiam† sanctam,
hostiam† immaculatam,
Panem† sanctum vitæ aeternæ
et Calicem † salutis perpetuæ.

[Therefore, O Lord, as we celebrate
the memorial of the blessed passion,
the resurrection from the underworld,

and the glorious ascension into heaven of Christ, Your Son,
Our Lord,
we, Your servants and Your holy people,
offer to Your glorious majesty from the gifts that You have
given us,
this pure† Victim,
this holy† Victim,
this spotless† Victim,
the holy Bread† of eternal life
and the Chalice† of everlasting salvation.]

In this place, we lovingly and reverently recall the passion of the Lord, His resurrection from the realm of death, and His ascension into the heavens. In the five signs of the cross which are made during this prayer, the five sacred wounds of Christ are represented—namely, two in His hands, two in His feet, and one in His side. The first three signs of the cross in the text above are made over both the Host and the chalice together. Through this we are taught to understand that the passion of Christ wounds the faithful and devout heart with the virtue of sacred *love*, that the resurrection of Christ strengthens the virtue of *faith*, and the glorious ascension of Christ animates with joy the virtue of *hope*.

The two remaining signs, made separately over the Host and the chalice, signify the two forms of immortality in which the just shall rejoice—namely, immortality of body and immortality of soul.

Indeed, the just and faithful who are illuminated by the wounds of Christ are made pure (or immaculate), and become the heirs of eternal life. In this eternal life, they attain perfect well-being and unassailable strength and happiness of both body and soul. This reality is beautifully signified in the words, "this pure Victim, this holy Victim, this spotless Victim, the holy Bread of eternal life and the Chalice of everlasting salvation."

For Christ is indeed the *pure* Victim, Who purifies His chosen; He is the *holy* Victim, Who makes holy His beloved; He is the *spotless* or immaculate Victim, Who purges away the stains of our sins. He is the Bread of eternal life, refreshing both angels and humans with His infinite goodness and bounty. And He is the chalice of everlasting salvation, inebriating with joy and exultation the heavens and the earth with His most precious Blood.

The Canon then proceeds to offer the following prayer, beseeched the Lord that He should graciously deign to accept the offerings made to Him:

Supra quæ propitio ac sereno vultu
respicere digneris; et accepta habere,
sicuti accepta habere dignatus es munera pueri tui justi Abel,
et sacrificium Patriarchæ nostri Abrahæ:
et quod tibi obtulit summus sacerdos tuus Melchisedech,
sanctum sacrificium, immaculatam hostiam.

[Deign to regard them with a gracious and serene countenance,

and to accept them, as You did deign to accept
the gifts of Your servant, Abel the just,
and the sacrifice of Abraham our Patriarch,
and that which Your high priest Melchizedek offered to You,
a holy sacrifice, a spotless victim.]

Note that in this text three persons from the Old Testament are mentioned—namely, Abel, Abraham, and Melchizedek. Each of these is a figure or foreshadowing of the passion of Christ, and each of these three also foreshadowed in their actions and lives the mystery of the Lord's Supper. Abel offered to God the firstborn lambs of his flocks, and similarly Christ, the firstborn of many brethren, offered Himself to the Father as an immaculate Lamb. Hence it was that John the Baptist proclaimed Him to be "the Lamb of God, Who takes away the sins of the world."[101] Similarly, the innocent Abel was cruelly killed by his wicked brother Cain. Thus it was that Christ was treacherously betrayed and killed by people of His own brothers—that is to say, by the people of His own nation and race.

Abraham obeyed God faithfully by his willingness to sacrifice his only begotten son, Isaac. And Christ, likewise, made Himself obedient to the Father even unto death, and freely gave His spirit into the hands of the Father.

---

[101] John 1:29, 36.

The ancient priest, Melchizedek, took bread and wine as an offering to God. And Scripture attests of him, "He was indeed a priest of God the Most High."[102]

And Christ Himself similarly offered sacrifice under the forms of wine and bread—though, in reality, it is Himself, in His Body and Blood, which He offers under these forms. And by making this sacrifice for us, He secured our eternal peace. And Melchizedek, foreshadowing this, is known as the prince of Salem, which means "the prince of Peace."[103] Yet if this title was given to Melchizedek in ancient times, it certainly applies more fully and more perfectly to Christ Himself.

In this part of the Canon, Christ is referred to under the names of these three Old Testament characters who prefigured Him: Abel, on account of His immaculate and spotless innocence; Abraham, on account of His faithful and perfect obedience, even to the point of offering his son as a victim; and Melchizedek, on account of His mercy and sanctity, in offering the sacrifice which achieves peace. Hence the words "a holy sacrifice, a spotless victim" follow here, imbued with this rich and mystic meaning.

---

[102] Genesis 14:18.

[103] Hebrews 7:2.

10

THE CANON OF THE MASS: PART VI

We read that it was Pope Saint Leo the Great[104] who, under the inspiration of God, added the words which follow to the text of the Canon. The prayer inserted by this great pontiff reads thus:

Supplices te rogamus, omnipotens Deus:
jube hæc perferri per manus sancti Angeli tui
in sublime altare tuum, in conspectu divinæ majestatis tuæ;
ut, quotquot, ex hac altaris participatione
sacrosanctum Filii tui Corpus† et Sanguinem† sumpserimus,
omni benedictione † cælesti et gratia repleamur.
Per eumdem Christum Dominum nostrum. Amen.

[In humble prayer we ask You, almighty God:
command that these (gifts)[105] be borne by
the hands of Your holy Angel

---

104 c. 400-461.

105 The word "gifts" is a translational insertion. The original Latin has only

to Your altar on high, in the sight of Your divine majesty,
so that all of us, who through this participation at the altar
receive the most holy Body† and Blood† of Your Son,
may be filled with every grace and heavenly† blessing.
Through the same Christ Our Lord. Amen.]

The profound bow of the priest at this point signifies the inclination of Christ, when, with an inclined head, He gave up His spirit to the Father. The faithful present at the Mass also ought to humble themselves devoutly at this point, and, through intimate and fervent sighs, to commend their own spirits to God. For the words of the prayer cited above, which Pope Leo the Great thoughtfully composed, are filled with ineffable and awesome mysteries.

Saint Gregory the Great affirms the power of these words, composed by his illustrious predecessor. For Saint Gregory writes, "Who amongst the faithful could doubt that at this point in the holy sacrifice of the Mass the heavens are thrown open upon hearing the voice of the priest, and the glorious choirs of the angels are all present. Indeed, at this point the highest is joined to the lowly, the celestial and earthly realms are united, and the visible and invisible realities become one!"[106] And in another place the same saint also writes, "At one and the same moment in time, as the angels in heaven rejoice before

---

the demonstrative adjective "*hæc,*" meaning "these."

[106] See St. Gregory the Great, *Dialogues*, IV.53.

the Body of Christ, so too is the very same Body seen by the eyes of the priest above the altar."

Aside from this mystical meaning, pertaining to the heavenly sacrament of Christ's Body, the words, "command that these be borne by the hands of Your holy Angel," can also be understood as relating to the prayers and supplications of the faithful. We read that when Tobias prayed, the angel carried his prayers into the presence of God. How much more when Christ, together with the priest, prays and presents the petitions and supplications of the holy Church in the Mass, shall the holy angel of God transmit these prayers to God, in the sight of His divine majesty! Hence it is that Saint Ambrose wrote, "Do not doubt that when Christ is offered as our holy sacrifice the angels of heaven are certainly there present."[107]

After the invocation to God to send His holy angel to bear our gifts and prayers, next follows, "to Your altar on high." This "altar on high" may be understood to be the Holy Trinity Himself. Taking this understanding of the "altar on high" to be the Holy Trinity, it is written, "You shall not ascend by steps to My altar."[108] This statement indicates that the equality of divine persons within the Trinity means that steps, which imply differences in highness and lowness, are not relevant here.[109] For

---

[107] See St. Ambrose, *On the Gospel of Luke,* I.

[108] Exodus 20:26.

[109] The point being made here is admittedly slightly difficult to grasp. Bonaventure's symbolic equation of the "altar on high" with the Holy Trinity, and his reference to the text about not approaching this altar (i.e., the

certain heretics have asserted that the Father is greater or higher than the Son, and these heretics may be said to attempt to ascend to the altar of God by means of steps. But such heretics are contradicted by the words of the Son, Who affirms, "I and the Father are one."[110]

And there are other heretics who maintain that the Holy Spirit is less than the Father and the Son. But their error is refuted by both the Father and the Son, for it is written, "The Spirit blows wherever He wishes,"[111] [implying the equality of the Spirit to the other persons of the Trinity]. And in the Gospel of John, it is stated very clearly that "the Spirit is God."[112] And in the Athanasian Creed, it is averred that "As the Father is, so also is the Son, and so also is the Holy Spirit."

Next follows, "In the sight of Your divine majesty." The Holy Trinity is described as the altar *on high*—that is, an altar so exalted as to transcend the comprehension of the merely human mind, or to be inaccessible to mortals. Nevertheless, Our Lord Jesus Christ, through His death, appeared before the Father, with Whom He is coeternal, on our behalf. It is as a consequence of this that "all of us, who through this participation at the altar receive the most holy Body and Blood of Your Son, [are] filled with every grace and heavenly blessing."

Trinity) by steps, is taken as refuting any idea of hierarchical distinctions within the Trinity.

[110] John 10:30.

[111] John 3:8.

[112] John 4:24.

It is to be noted that the sign of the cross is made three times during this prayer.[113] In the first two of these signs, we signify that it is the Lord alone Who can impart to us chastity of body and purity of soul, for the Body and Blood of Christ represent respectively these elements of the human being. Accordingly, Moses wrote, "The soul of man is in his blood."[114]

The third sign of the cross [coinciding with the words "every grace and heavenly blessing"] is made by the priest, beginning at his face, and extending downwards to his chest. While these words are being said, his head is inclined, signifying the death of Christ, Who "with an inclined head, gave up His spirit."[115]

This memorial of Christ upon the cross is profoundly significant here. For Saint Ambrose says that it was while Christ, the author of all piety, was thus hanging upon the cross that He assigned what was due and fitting to each. To the apostles, He assigned the vocation of undergoing persecution; to His other disciples, He gave heavenly peace; to the Father, He commended His immortal spirit; to the Blessed Virgin, He bequeathed the beloved disciple as a guardian; and to the repentant thief, He promised entrance into paradise. And to every Christian, He assigned his own particular cross to carry. Therefore, let us devoutly take up the cross which He has assigned us!

---

[113] The Latin text that follows mentions only the first and third signs of the cross, which seems to be an error. The paragraph that follows restores in complete form what seems to be the intended sense.

[114] Leviticus 17:11.

[115] John 19:30.

In making the two signs of the cross which are made over the Host and the chalice, we signify that we are liberated from the hold of death, in regard to both the body and the soul. But this liberation depends upon our perseverance in the confession of the Faith, which is represented by the third sign of the cross. For, "if we suffer with Him," as Saint Paul writes, "we shall surely reign with Him!"[116]

The three signs of the cross that occur in this text may also be understood in yet another symbolic way, as representing the various stages that Our Lord underwent during His passion and death. The first sign of the cross [made over the Host] symbolizes the scourging of His Body with whips. The second sign of the cross [made over the chalice] represents the flowing forth of His sacred Blood from His wounds. The third sign of the cross [made by the priest over his face, and extending down to his chest] symbolizes the veiling of the face and body of Jesus in the burial sheets.

[116] Romans 8:17 and 2 Timothy 2:12.

11

THE CANON OF THE MASS: PART VII

Just as Christ, when He was about to depart from this world, earnestly commended His spirit to the Father, so it is fitting that, as we draw toward the end of the Canon of the Mass, we should commend to almighty God the souls of all the faithful departed. Hence it is that that Canon continues with the text:

> Remember also, Lord, Your servants (N. and N.)
> who have gone before us with the sign of faith
> and rest in the sleep of peace.
> Grant them, O Lord, we pray,
> and all who sleep in Christ,
> a place of refreshment, light, and peace.
> Through the same Christ Our Lord. Amen.

It is to be observed that Holy Mother Church prays, through the person of the priest, not only for the living but also for the dead. She does this firmly believing that the most precious Blood of Christ was shed not only to redeem the living, but even to release the dead from the torments of the underworld and the pains of purgatory. The expression, "who have gone before us with the sign of faith," refers to all those who are imbued with true charity, for this is indeed the sign of faith; and in this, those who are truly faithful may be distinguished from the unfaithful. Concerning this liberation of the departed from torments, the prophet [Zachariah] wrote, "And You, [Christ], through the Blood of Your covenant, have drawn forth those enchained in the depths of the abyss."[117]

Of course, it should not be imagined that we are praying for those souls who have actually been eternally condemned to hell. Indeed, of such souls, Saint Augustine once wrote, "If I knew for certain that my own father had been condemned to hell, from which there is no release, I would no more pray for him that I would for the devil!"[118] Rather, we pray only for those who "rest in the sleep of peace"—that is, for those who were not separated from the Church by heresy or unrepented and grave sin, but nevertheless may still carry upon their conscience various faults and offences. At this point, the priest ought to pray first of all for his own [deceased] father and mother, and afterwards other deceased persons in his care. But he should do this only mentally, not specifically mentioning them by name.

Next follows a prayer for "all who sleep in Christ." The dead who are said to "sleep in Christ" are the same as those who

---

[117] Zachariah 9:11.

[118] See St. Augustine, *The City of God*, XI:24.

are described as having "died in Christ" in the book of Revelation.[119] For these, we ask that they be granted "a place of refreshment, light, and peace." The "light" mentioned here is Christ Himself, Who is described as "the light of the world."[120] He is also the light of all the living [that is, both those living in this mortal life and those who have entered the life beyond death]. Hence we read in the psalm, "May I please God in the light of the living."[121]

The next prayer is made for ourselves. The text proceeds thus:

> To us, also, Your servants, who, though sinners,
> hope in Your abundant mercies,
> graciously grant some share
> and fellowship with Your holy Apostles and Martyrs:
> with John [the Baptist], Stephen,
> Matthias, Barnabas,
> Ignatius, Alexander,
> Marcellinus, Peter,
> Felicity, Perpetua,
> Agatha, Lucy,
> Agnes, Cecilia, Anastasia
> and all Your Saints;
> admit us, we beseech You,
> into their company,
> not weighing our merits,

---

119 Revelation 14:13.

120 John 8:12.

121 Psalm 55:13.

but granting us Your pardon,
through Christ Our Lord.
Through Whom
You continue to make all these good things, O Lord;
You sanctify them, fill them with life,
bless them, and bestow them upon us.

When we say, "To us, also, Your servants, who, though sinners," we are speaking in accordance with the precept of Saint John the Apostle, who writes, "If we say that we have no sin, we deceive ourselves and the truth is not within us."[122] And we read similarly in the book of Job, "There is no man who has not sinned, even if he is only an infant and has been on earth for only one day!"[123] There are many holy people who, by the mercy of God, are able to avoid mortal sin, but to find any person who is able to live without venial sin is hardly possible![124]

Next follows the description of ourselves as those who "hope in Your abundant mercies." If the repentant thief hanging from the cross was able to merit the mercy of Christ, why should genuinely contrite and repentant Christians doubt that they will also obtain such mercy? This contrition here is not expressed in words only, but also by a striking of the chest with the right hand. The right hand is used to symbolize this repentant thief, for it was at the right side of Our Lord that he was crucified.

---

[122] 1 John 1:8.

[123] Cf. Job 14.

[124] The exception to this is, of course, the Blessed Virgin Mary, who was conceived and lived without any stain of sin at all.

He openly confessed his guilt with true contrition, and said to his fellow thief (who hung from the cross on the left side of Jesus), "We have only received what we deserved." But Our Lord reassured Him, promising him a wonderful inheritance in the following words: "Amen, I say to you: This day you shall be with Me in paradise."[125]

Next, we earnestly beseech the Lord that He will "graciously grant [us] some share and fellowship with [His] holy apostles and martyrs." Saint John Chrysostom offers the opinion that the repentant thief will be granted one of the most exalted places in the kingdom of heaven, for he professed Christ to possess dominion over the celestial realm, whereas the apostle Peter had denied Him three times.[126] From this, we may conclude that sinners who sincerely and fervently repent attain to greater merit than those who may lead relatively innocent lives, but remain always tepid and uncommitted in their declaration of the Faith. Now, at this point in time, the Blessed Virgin Mary and all the apostles were still alive on earth. John the Baptist and the patriarchs were still in limbo, for Christ had not yet descended to the world of the dead to liberate them from their confinement. Thus, this repentant thief gained admission to the kingdom of heaven before any of these, for Our Lord said to Him, "*This day* you will be with Me in paradise." And this

---

[125] Luke 23:41, 43.

[126] See St. John Chrysostom, *On the Cross and the Repentant Thief*, Homily II:2.

paradise is to be found wherever Christ is—for wherever He is, there is joy, and paradise, and light, and peace, and delight!

For Christ is indeed the "true light."[127] He illuminates the heavens and spreads radiance through the celestial Jerusalem, as is stated in Revelation: "The Lamb Himself will be the light of the city."[128] There all the saints rejoice for endless ages!

And so it is that we devoutly petition to be granted "some share and fellowship with Your saints, apostles and martyrs."[129] Some commentators understand the John mentioned here to be John the Baptist, whereas others believe it is John the Evangelist. Now, John the Evangelist had already been named at the beginning of the Canon with the other apostles. But, according to those who believe that he is mentioned here again, they opine that he merited to be named twice in the Canon, for attaining the double sanctity of apostleship and holy virginity.[130] This special privilege reflects the particular affection which Jesus had for this apostle, whom He regarded as His own beloved son, and entrusted lovingly to the care of His Mother.

Concerning the female martyrs who are mentioned at this point, it is to be noted that Saints Felicity and Perpetua, who are

---

[127] John 1:9.

[128] Revelation 21:23.

[129] This is taking a slightly different sense from the usual English translation of the Latin text: *"cum tuis sanctis apostolis et martyribus."*

[130] It is to be observed that the traditional Latin text of the Roman Canon mentions only John here, with "John the Baptist" being added in the *Novus Ordo*. Ancient traditions hold that Saint John the Apostle was very young, and a virgin.

listed first, are the only two who were married women, whereas all the others were virgin-martyrs.[131] The reason for their names appearing first may simply be that they were chronologically the earliest of those listed. But it may also be to highlight a point made by Saint Augustine—namely, that virginity in itself, unless accompanied by humility, does not ensure sanctity. However, virginity, if cultivated with true humility and piety, will certainly merit a higher place in the kingdom of heaven.[132] At this point in the Canon, martyrs, virgins, and proclaimers of the Faith all appear, representing the whole communion of saints, as is reflected in the words, "and all Your saints."

An invocation of the entire Trinity is to be found in the text:

> Through Whom [i.e., God the Son]
> You [God the Father] continue to make
> all these good things, O Lord;
> You [God the Holy Spirit] sanctify them,
> fill them with life,
> bless them, and bestow them upon us.

This shows that it is not merely the priest who consecrates the sacred offerings and achieves the transubstantiation into the Body and Blood of Christ, but the whole Trinity. This Trinitarian dynamic is likewise embodied in the words "*sanctificas,*

---

[131] It is believed that St. Anastasia, who is mentioned with these female martyrs in the Canon, was also married. It is possible that Bonaventure may have overlooked this.

[132] See St. Augustine, *On Holy Virginity*, 45.

vivificas, benedicis" ["You sanctify them, give them life, bless them. . ."].

These three words also signify the three days during which Christ remained in the world of the dead, and rested from the work of salvation He had accomplished by His passion and death. We read that "unless a grain of wheat" [that is, Christ Our Lord] "falls to the ground and dies, it remains but a single grain."[133] But because this holy grain *has* fallen to the ground and died, it springs up anew. By His death, Christ sanctified; by His resurrection, He has given life; and by the blessing of the bread from heaven, He has graciously blessed us.

Hence, this formula concludes with "and bestow them upon us." In this, we indicate that Christ bestows sanctification, vivification, and blessing through this sacrament. For by His Body, we are sanctified; by His Blood, we are made to live; and by consuming both in a worthy manner, we are made eternally blessed!

---

[133] John 12:24–25.

12

THE DOXOLOGY, LORD'S PRAYER, AND FRACTION RITE

Next follows the doxology, which concludes the Canon. It is worded thus:

> Through Him,† and with Him,† and in Him,†
> O God, almighty Father, †
> in the unity of the Holy Spirit, †
> all glory and honor are Yours,
> for ever and ever. Amen.

It is to be noted that during the words "Through Him, and with Him, and in Him," the sign of the cross is made three times. These commemorate the three days during which Christ rested amongst the dead. They also signify the threefold purposes of His passion and resurrection—namely, the restoration of the heavens, the reparation of the earth, and the redemption of those souls who had been confined to the underworld.

It may also be understood as symbolizing the Trinity, Who is invoked in this doxology. In the Father is represented the *authority* of God; in the Son is shown the *equality* of the Divine Persons; and in the Holy Spirit is manifested the perfect *communion* between these Divine Persons.

While the words, "Through Him, and with Him, and in Him," are being pronounced, the Host is held above the chalice, and, the sign of the cross is made with the Host over the chalice of the Blood. By this is symbolized that death has been definitively overcome by Christ, and life restored, and everlasting glory bestowed.

The closing words of the doxology, "for ever and ever," are spoken by the priest in a loud and clear voice, and the chalice and Host are both elevated above the altar, with the Host being held above the chalice. This action signifies how the sadness of the apostles over the death of the Lord was dispelled from their hearts when the wonderful news of the Resurrection was first announced to them.

Next follows an invitation to prayer, with the word "*Oremus.*"[134] It continues thus:

> At the Savior's command
> and formed by divine teaching,
> we dare to say:
> Our Father. . . .

[134] "Let us pray." This is not included in the *Novus Ordo* form, which proceeds immediately to the introduction to the Lord's Prayer.

Thus it is that, strengthened by the mercy of God, we arise from the dark death of sin. We do this with firm resolution and hope not to fall into it once again, just like Christ, Who "rising from the dead now dies no more."[135] May we flee from the horrible demon of sin, and turn to the mercy and sweetness of the Lord's paternal mercy instead!

For God did not disdain to be known as "the Father of all" and "the Father of mercies and the God of all consolation."[136] And we are about to address God, the merciful Father, as "our Father." We dare to do this, having been "formed by divine teaching." It was the Son Himself Who taught this, Who is coequal with the Father. In instructing us to address *His* Father as "*our* Father," He has bestowed upon us the dignity of being His brothers. He is the Son of God by nature; we are sons of God by divine grace. It is for this reason that we dare to say, "Our Father Who art in heaven."

The Lord's Prayer is then recited, in which we petition God for our daily bread. This "daily bread" will be provided in the sacred Host, which is the very Body of Christ and the food of angels. Those assembled respond with a confident affirmation of "Amen." According to Saint Jerome, this is a Hebrew word, carrying the meaning "Let it be so, most truly and faithfully!" Thus, at this point, it is as if the Church declares to the celebrating priest, "O reverend priest, let everything which you

---

[135] Romans 6:9.

[136] 2 Corinthians 1:4.

have requested in this prayer be fulfilled and come to pass, most truly and most faithfully!"

Next follows the prayer:

> Deliver us, we beseech You, O Lord, from all evils,
> past, present, and to come;
> and by the intercession of the blessed and glorious,
>   Mary ever virgin, Mother of God,
> together with Your blessed apostles
>   Peter and Paul, and Andrew,
> and all the saints,
> mercifully grant peace in our days:
> that through the help of Your mercy
>   we may always be free from sin,
> and safe from all distress.
> Through the same Jesus Christ, Your Son, Our Lord,
> Who lives and reigns with You
>   in the unity of the Holy Spirit,
> God, for ever and ever. Amen.[137]

At this point, a third commemoration of the saints is made. The entire communion of saints is included, and are represented by the mention of the Blessed Virgin Mary, and the apostles Saints Peter, Paul, and Andrew. For sainthood is attained either through chastity, or strength of virtue, humility, or by bravely fighting for justice. In the Blessed Virgin, chastity is

---

[137] It is to be noted that this prayer, which follows the Lord's Prayer, is abbreviated in the *Novus Ordo*.

represented; in Saint Peter, strength of virtue; in Saint Paul, humility; and in Saint Andrew, courageous battle for the truth, even unto death itself.[138]

In these words, we implore the Lord that He "mercifully grant peace in our days." The practice of praying for peace was instituted by Saint Paul himself, when he said, "I ask that first of all should come prayers, petitions, requests and thanksgiving, for all people, for kings, and for those who occupy high positions, so that we may lead a quiet and tranquil life in all piety."[139] Therefore, the Church diligently prays for peace and good order, even in a secular and temporal sense, so that she may not be impeded or drawn away from her spiritual peace.

Next follows the petition "that through the help of Your mercy [in respect to both interior and exterior things] we may always be free from sin, and safe from all distress." We suffer distress if we are burdened with mortal sin. For such sins make the human heart blind. When blinded by sin, we are "in distress," for our free and rational will no longer governs us, and we are distanced from divine grace. It is therefore fitting that the priest prays that we may be kept safe from such sin and distress, through Him Who alone is able to save us—that is, "through the same Jesus Christ [. . .] Our Lord."

---

[138] The identification of these saints with particular virtues seems to relate to the meaning of their names—*Petrus*, meaning 'a rock' (i.e., strength), *Paulus*, meaning 'small' (i.e., humble), and *Andreas* meaning 'manly' (i.e., courageous.)

[139] 1 Timothy 2:1–2.

But before the priest pronounces these words, he uncovers the chalice, and raises the Body of Christ (that is, the consecrated Host) above the chalice and breaks it into three pieces. One of these parts he places into the chalice, while the other two he reserves. But before he places the one part into the chalice, he says in a clear voice, "The Peace of the Lord." And he makes the sign of the cross three times with the particle of the Body of Christ over the chalice, before placing it in the chalice.[140]

What this signifies, we shall briefly reflect upon. According to Pope Sergius [I],[141] "The threefold division of the consecrated Host signifies the Body of Christ in three senses. The portion of the consecrated Host which is placed in the chalice is the Body of Christ which lay in the tomb and rose from death. The part which is consumed by the priest is the Body of Christ as it walked among the living on this earth. The part which is reserved on the altar until the end of the Mass is the Body of Christ in the communion of the saints, who are mystically members of His same Body, and who shall remain at rest until the end of the world."

Although the physical form of the consecrated bread is divided in this threefold manner, the Body of Christ, in its divine substance and essence, is not divided—for the Deity is, by its very nature, indivisible. Augustine speaks about the breaking

---

[140] The practice which Bonaventure has described here is very similar (but not identical) to that of the Tridentine Mass. The *Novus Ordo* Mass is substantially different at this point.

[141] c. 650-701.

of the consecrated Host, when he says, "When Christ is consumed in the Eucharist, He refreshes and nourishes those who consume Him. But He Himself is in no way diminished or broken."[142] And Christ rebuked His disciples when they understood the eating of His flesh in a purely physical sense.[143] The Body of Christ is broken and divided only in appearances and visible form, but not in its essence and substance.

For the Body of Christ, though truly present, is veiled under *accidents,* or perceptible characteristics. These perceptible characteristics include color, flavor, size, and shape. For the *substance* or reality of the bread and wine was truly cut off (*resecatur*) [and replaced] by the [substance or reality of] the Body and Blood of Christ, by virtue of the consecration. Nevertheless, the *accidents,* or perceptible qualities, of the bread and wine remain unchanged. For if the perceptible qualities of the bread and wine were also changed into flesh and blood, those present would certainly be shocked and terrified. Thus, the miracle of the change of substance without any change of perceptible qualities has been divinely ordained in all wisdom, out of kind consideration of our human fragility.

The division of the consecrated Host into three parts may also be understood to signify the three elements or aspects of Christ—namely, His divinity, His Body, and His soul. The one particle that is placed into the chalice signifies that, in His

---

[142] See Augustine, *Sermon 132.*

[143] Cf. John 6:53–64.

Body, Christ was able to endure the passion and to die. But the other two parts, which are not placed in the chalice, signify His soul (which is immortal) and His divinity (which is impassible, or not subject to suffering).

The division of the consecrated Host may also be interpreted as representing the Holy Trinity. The particle that is placed in the chalice may be understood to symbolize the Son. For, although the Trinity is indivisible in His works and will, nevertheless, it was only the Son Who was made flesh. Thus, the other two portions, which are not placed in the chalice, signify the Father and the Holy Spirit, Who were not made flesh.

The paradox of this division of the indivisible Trinity is reflected in the words of the priest. For as he breaks the Host, he says, "Through Our Lord Jesus Christ, Who lives and reigns forever and ever." In doing this, it is as if he says, "Behold, I appear to divide the indivisible! And in the same mysterious way, though Christ died in His humility, nevertheless He lives and reigns eternally through His divinity. And if He was seen to depart from the Father in His incarnation, still, He remains always perfectly united to the Father in His immortal and divine substance."

And the priest also breaks the consecrated Host when he says, "in the unity of the Holy Spirit." In doing this, it is as if he proclaims, "Though we read that the Holy Spirit overshadowed the most Blessed Virgin when the Son was conceived, nevertheless this same Holy Spirit proceeds eternally from the Father and the

Son, and is never separated from them in substance and operation. Rather, the Holy Trinity, the one and only God, remains undivided *per omnia sæcula sæculorum*—for ever and ever!"

The division of the Host into three parts may also be understood as reflecting the threefold division of the Church, which is truly the mystical Body of Christ. Firstly, there is the Head of the Body, which is Christ Himself, the firstborn of the newly arisen humanity. The other members of the Body (which are the remainder of the Church) form the other two parts—namely, the Church Triumphant, or the victorious souls of the blessed in the kingdom of heaven; and the Church Militant, or those who are still fighting faithfully in this earthly life.[144] The two parts which are not placed in the chalice may be understood as Christ [the Head of the Church], together with the Church Triumphant. But the particle which is placed in the chalice represents the Church Militant, that is still immersed in the striving and struggles of this life.

It is also possible to interpret the threefold division of the Host as a representation of the three states of life of those within the Church—namely, virgins, widows, and those who are married. The two parts which are reserved and not placed in

---

[144] It is to be noted that Bonaventure's division of the Church into three parts here (Christ, the Church Triumphant, and the Church Militant) does not precisely correspond with the division which has now become customary (the Church Triumphant, the Church Militant, and the Church Suffering). However, this second threefold way of considering the Church will appear a little later in this chapter.

the chalice represent those two states which are celibate—that is, virginity and widowhood. This in in accordance with the apostle's [Saint Paul's] grouping of these two celibate states together, when he says, "Virgins and those who do not have husbands think of those things which are of the Lord."[145] The third part, which is placed into the chalice, signifies those who live in the married state. Of these, St. Paul says that "those who are married must consider the affairs of the world."[146] Likewise, he says that married persons are bound to suffer from tribulations and stress of various kinds. The Host is thus offered for all three classes of Christian persons. It is offered for virgins and widows, that they may faithfully persevere in their condition of celibacy; and for married men and women, that they may not be overcome by the trials and demands which pertain to their state of life.

Another possible interpretation of the division of the Host into three parts is described in the following verses:

> The Body of Christ is divided into three,
> The part in the chalice is for the living,
> The part not placed in the chalice is for the saints,
> And the third part is for the justification of the sinful.[147]

This should be understood as indicating that the first part of the consecrated Host is offered for Christians who are still

---

145 1 Corinthians 7:34.

146 1 Corinthians 7:34.

147 It seems that this verse was in circulation in Bonaventure's time.

living this earthly life, and who are struggling with the trials and tribulations of the life of this world—this is the Church Militant. The part of the Host offered for them is to obtain the mercy and grace of God to assist them in the ordeals, challenges, and temptations which they must face. The second part, which is not placed in the chalice, is offered for the praise and veneration of the saints, or those blessed souls who already rejoice in the glory and joy of the kingdom of heaven—which is the Church Triumphant. The other part is offered to assist the souls who are in purgatory, who are suffering in remittance for their sins, and still await the rewards and delights of heaven. These souls in purgatory form the Church Suffering. The part of the Body of Christ offered on their behalf is to hasten their liberation from the torments they still undergo, and to bring them relief and refreshment.

13

THE EXCHANGE OF PEACE AND THE *AGNUS DEI*

As the particle of the Body of Christ is placed into the chalice, the priest says in a clear voice, "The Peace of the Lord." By these words, in combination with the threefold division of the consecrated Host, the threefold peace which Christ left His disciples is signified. This threefold peace consists of temporal or earthly peace, peace in one's heart, and eternal peace.

The priest says, "Peace be with you," to which those present respond, "And with your spirit." In these words, it is as if the congregation is saying to the priest, "You have wished peace for us: may this same peace which you desire for us remain also with *your* spirit, insofar as you partake of the divine mysteries. May you be filled with all spiritual joy!"

The threefold peace that is signified here is symbolized in the three kisses of the altar, which are made by the priest during the course of the Mass—namely, those at the beginning, in the middle, and at the end. For when Christ was born in human flesh, He brought a new era of peace into this world, and so granted us *temporal* peace. This peace is designated by the first kiss of the altar, which the priest makes at the beginning of the Mass. The second form of peace is internal peace, or the peace within one's own heart and conscience. This second form of peace is represented by the second kiss of the alar, which the priest makes when he pronounces the words, "In humble prayer we ask You, almighty God. . . ." For when Christ died for us upon the Cross, He reconciled us to God and to the holy angels, and thereby restored peace to our hearts and consciences. To confirm this peace, He allowed His own chest and side to be opened with a lance, so that we may enter into His own perfect peace of heart. The third form of peace, which is eternal peace, is symbolized in the final kiss of the altar, which the priest makes at the end of the Mass. Christ opened this peace up for us when, having fulfilled all that was written in the Law and the Prophets, He ascended in triumph to the Father in heaven. Similarly, with the sacrifice of the Mass being completed and fulfilled, this final kiss of the altar represents the ultimate and everlasting peace which is promised to us in the kingdom of heaven.

It is to be noted that from the Lord's Prayer until the end of the Mass, different parts are vocalized in different ways. Some are said in an undertone by the priest, whereas others are sung by him in a clear voice, and others are sung or spoken by the choir or assembly. This reflects that after Christ had risen from the tomb, His modes of presence were varied. Sometimes He appeared clearly and visibly before the apostles to dispel from their hearts the silence of sorrow. But at other times, His physical presence was not visible, and it was as if He vanished from their sight. For it is read that during the forty days between the Resurrection and the Ascension, Christ appeared to His disciples some ten times; but on other occasions, He completely hid Himself from view. This variability is reflected in the varied tone in which the words of the Mass are presented (sometimes clearly and perceptibly, and at other times in such a manner that they are inaudible to the assembly) from the Lord's Prayer until the dismissal. For this portion of the Mass may be understood as symbolically corresponding to the time from the Lord's resurrection from the dead until His glorious ascension into heaven.

Next follows the "Lamb of God." This was introduced by Pope Sergius [I], to be sung with the utmost devotion during the breaking of the consecrated Host. The word *agnus* ("lamb") is derived from *agnoscendo* ("knowing"), for a lamb knows its own mother, simply by hearing her bleating. Thus it was that Christ, the Lamb of God, truly and completely *knew* His Father through obedience. He similarly knew His blessed Mother through His reverence and love, as He commended her to His own beloved disciple, John, as He faced death. Christ is indeed the true Lamb of God, Who alone was perfectly innocent; and it was on account of this perfect innocence that He was so cruelly killed. Thus it is that the Church sings out, "They shall mourn for Him as for an only begotten Son, for the innocent God has been killed."[148]

We customarily sing *Agnus Dei* ("Lamb of God") three times. In doing this, it is as if we proclaim, "Lamb of God," Who knew the Father through perfect obedience, "have mercy on us; Lamb of God," Who knew Your Mother through reverence and love, "have mercy on us; Lamb of God, Who take away the sins of the world" through Your immaculate innocence, "grant us peace." The triple singing of the *Agnus Dei* may also be understood as a fervent beseeching that we be liberated from all evils and sins—past, present, and future.

Following this, a kiss of peace is exchanged amongst those present. This was introduced by Pope Innocent (I).[149] This action is a sign that it behooves us to cleanse ourselves of all bitterness of heart. For if we are in conflict, animosity, and discord with each other, we cannot be perfectly united as the Body of Christ. This is expressed by the apostle Saint John when he writes, "Whoever hates his brother is a murderer, and we know that all who hate their brethren do not have a part in the kingdom of God."[150] Let us therefore hold peace with our neighbors, and peace among ourselves, by being united with each other in sincerely loving Christ! In this manner, with the grace of Our Lord Jesus Christ, shall we attain the celestial peace which endures forever.

---

[148] See Zachariah 12:10.

[149] 378–417.

[150] 1 John 3:15.

14

THE PRIESTLY RECEPTION OF COMMUNION, THE PRAYER AFTER COMMUNION, AND THE DISMISSAL

Once the Canon of the Mass is concluded, the priest then reverently consumes the most holy Body of Christ. Some priests do this by hand, whereas others consume it directly from the paten. Those who choose this latter mode interpret their action as signifying that they receive the Body of Christ in the *breadth* of God's charity, which is symbolized by the broad form of the paten. Meanwhile the Communion antiphon is sung, emulating the joy of the disciples as they announced the resurrection of the Lord among themselves.

After this follows a prayer. This prayer, made by the priest on behalf of the assembly, represents the eleven disciples as they were filled with joy upon seeing the Risen Christ. Similarly, it also symbolizes Christ Himself, Who is always engaged in prayer on our behalf in heaven, and displaying His healing wounds and the signs of His saving passion to the Father in supplication for mercy for us sinners.

Finally, the priest says to the assembly, "Go forth: the Mass is ended," and he blesses all the people present. This signifies that when Christ returns in judgment, He shall bless His own faithful people. By virtue of this blessing, they shall then go forth into the celestial dwelling places prepared for them, of which we read in the Gospel of John: "In My Father's house there are many dwelling places."[151] To these blessed and glorious dwelling places may Christ, Who is our supreme High Priest, graciously lead us; Who lives and reigns with the Father and the Holy Spirit forever and ever! Amen.

---

[151] John 14:2.

SAINT BONAVENTURE'S PRAYER BEFORE RECEIVING COMMUNION

My Lord, Who are You, and who am I, that I should presume to take You within the foulness of my own wretched body and soul? Why have You created me, so that I should commit this detestable offence against Your Majesty? A thousand years of weeping would not suffice to make anyone worthy to receive such a noble Sacrament. How much more, then, am I unworthy, since I fall into sin every single day, and seem utterly unable to correct myself!

But Your compassion is infinitely greater than my own wretchedness.

Hence, placing all my confidence in Your mercy, I dare to consume You, my Lord and my God. *Amen.*

SAINT BONAVENTURE'S PRAYER AFTER MASS

O most sweet Jesus Christ, pierce the innermost parts of my soul with the wound of Your most delightful and saving love and with true and apostolic charity, so that it may languish and melt with love and longing for You! May it yearn for You, and rest in You in the courtrooms of Your house. May it desire to be dissolved completely, and thus to be forever united with You!

Grant that my soul may eagerly thirst for the food of angels, the refreshment of holy souls, and our true daily bread, having within itself all sweetness and delight.

May my heart always long for You, Whom the angels desire to gaze upon. May it thirst for You, the font of life and the font of wisdom, the font of eternal light, and the stream of all happiness. May it desire You, and seek You, and find You! May it mediate upon You and undertake all its works solely for the glory of Your divine name.

May You always be my hope, my faith, my riches, my delight, my happiness, my joy, my peace, and my tranquility, my refuge, my help, my inheritance, my treasure! In You, may my heart and my mind be constantly, firmly, and unshakably rooted. *Amen.*